PERFECT PLATES

PERFECT

5

IN FIVE INGREDIENTS

PLATES

JOHN WHAITE

Photography by Helen Cathcart
Kyle Books

FOR WINNIE AND FDR

Acknowledgements

There are many people I would like to thank for help and advice over the years, but to ensure I don't heavily offend, I'm keeping this list of folk entirely relevant to this book. And I shan't gush, because I can't stand sickliness. So, in no particular order:

To: Kyle, Judith, Sophie, all at Kyle Books, Helen, Linda, River, Kinga, Nicole, Frances, Holly, Rosie, Jonny, Laura, and Paul

"I can no other answer make but thanks, and thanks, and ever thanks."
William Shakespeare.

With love and gratitude.

First published in Great Britain in 2016 by
Kyle Books, an imprint of Kyle Cathie Ltd
192-198 Vauxhall Bridge Road
London SW1V 1DX
general.enquiries@kylebooks.com
www.kylebooks.co.uk

10 9 8 7 6 5 4 3 2 1

ISBN 978 0 85783 351 8

Text © 2016 John Whaite
Design © 2016 Kyle Books
Photography © 2016 Helen Cathcart

Designer: Paul Atkins
Photographer: Helen Cathcart
Food Stylist: Nicole Herft
Props Stylist: Linda Berlin
Project Editor: Sophie Allen
Editorial Assistant: Hannah Coughlin
Production: Nic Jones, Gemma John and Lisa Pinnell

A Cataloguing in Publication record for this title is available from the British Library.

Colour reproduction by ALTA, London
Printed and bound in Slovenia by DZS Grafik d.o.o

CONTENTS

INTRODUCTION

In all honesty, I was dreading writing this book. The premise of the title wasn't something I ever thought possible: that I could produce delicious meals with only a limited number of ingredients. In fact, the very thought filled me with horror; in my eyes more is more, and I've never been one for frugality. You may wonder why I came up with the idea for this book. I too wondered that many a time over the course of the recipe testing, but as well as being a devout subscriber to immoderation, I am also a sucker for a challenge.

It transpired that my fears were entirely irrational: when I began to pare back recipes and use fewer ingredients I was reminded of the uncomplicated flavours of my childhood. I remembered my Auntie Mary handing me a punnet of cherry tomatoes. The smell of the tomatoes was so sweetly intense that all they needed was a drizzle of peppery olive oil and a few torn shreds of basil to complete them. It wasn't necessary to lob a load of other components thoughtlessly at the plate; it was unassumingly perfect in its simplicity.

That idea was something I wanted to return to, so the initial stage in writing this book was to define what perfection in food is. But to understand even that I needed to ask myself: what is the ultimate aim of preparing food? Clearly, we've long since evolved from the primitive notion of 'food as fuel'. You only need to look to the abuse of food and vocabulary that is 'molecular gastronomy' to know that today food is about entertainment. We throw dinner parties to entertain as much as we do to catch up with friends but, let's face it, we all want to serve up an impressive spread because we love a bit of glitzy one-upmanship on our peers.

Sometimes we cook for attention; chefs and cooks are often the most glory-hunting individuals on the planet. But surely you yourself can't deny that social praise for a toothsome batch of flapjacks brings an insatiable urge for more? My mother, in particular, is well versed in this little game. After a meal cooked by her, no matter how delicious it was, she will always apologise for 'letting us down'. She knows quite well how excellent her food is, but she loves us to make even more fuss over it. Poor Linda.

Really, I don't suppose the question of perfect food at home, on a day-to-day basis, is much considered in any depth. I think that's just because food is simply a part of who we are; it's a visceral appreciation. Food at home isn't perfect, and that is what is perfect about it. That's not to say that it is unconsidered or taken for granted – though it can be – it's just that what we eat throughout our lives can, and does, depend heavily on what we are fed as children. We know what we enjoy, and that is something we can inherit. The food that we love stays with us as we grow up, without us really heralding or fussing over it all that much. I know that nothing I ever make for my partner will compare to his mother's corned beef hash – a fact that I have ambitiously but futilely resisted for all too long.

For me, all of that highlights what perfect food is: simple ingredients that bring a reassuring familiarity, prepared with rustic sentiment. There's nothing elaborate needed; there's no urge to discover deeply complex flavours by way of lengthy processes and specialist equipment – 'imperfect plates', I guess, would have been a more suitable title for this book. There will always be the temptation to throw something else onto the plate, but you shouldn't be afraid to resist. Coco Chanel said that before you leave the house you should remove one item of clothing. If anyone had ever tried to apply that concept to food, I'd have unfriended and blacklisted that person for life. But now, I completely get it: perfection is found in familiar simplicity.

The Premise and the Promise

This is a cookbook in which each recipe uses just five main ingredients. Your 'free passes' are what I would call 'the Essentials': oil, butter, salt, pepper and water. They don't count in the five main ingredients as I'd expect most people to already have them in their cupboards and fridge.

Now, I'm sure we'd all love to spend our day trundling around an idyllic farmers' market, soaking up the sweet scent of vine tomatoes and the boisterous pungency of towering stacks of artisan cheeses. I dream about testing ingredient after ingredient, revisiting each two or three times before deciding on my favourite, but that just isn't realistic; the scales of the work–life balance are most definitely dishonest. With that in mind, I've used ingredients here that are, for the most part, available in both supermarkets and specialist food markets. Both are fabulous, both are necessary, so the choice is entirely yours.

I'm stepping back from the currently complicated to let the ingredients do the talking; if we really needed all this elaborate molecular gastronomy we'd have starved and shuffled off this mortal coil a long time ago.

With just five main ingredients, plates of food can be created. That is the premise. The promise is that the food will be perfect – not fancy, elaborate or technical, just perfect.

MORNING PLATES

LAVISH WEEKEND BRUNCHES

Before you even begin to browse the recipes on the following pages, I feel the need to urge you to do so with the chapter's subtitle in mind: lavish weekend brunches. Many of the recipes here are decadent, but that's because they aren't intended to be something you'd eat every single morning. Well, you could, but who knows where that would get you? And besides, the origin of these indulgent recipes is rooted more in the social, joyous sort of breakfast rather than a lonesome, reluctant nibble on some stale cornflakes. You made it through the night – surely that's a reason to celebrate?

Joking aside, of course there are some more balanced recipes, too, and those are the ones that I make time and time again. It's just that I like to think weekend mornings are used properly. Throughout the week most of us are frantic in our lives. We are slaves to the alarm clock and the upward out-of-bed struggle is relentless. So when the weekend comes, I'd much rather have a lie-in before I haul myself into the kitchen to calmly get on with some idle pottering.

What I'd truly like to do every weekend is spend an entire morning with friends or family, and food. I once went for brunch with a group of mates and it lasted for five hours – admittedly, a bottomless supply of prosecco did fuel the fire, but that too can be arranged at home, can't it?

These recipes are the types of things you'd do as a breakfast buffet for your mates, as much as they are fitting treats for family brunches. However you view the recipes, and whatever occasion you cook them for, the real provenance of this entire chapter is found in that trite old cliché: breakfast is the most important meal of the day – because for me and mine, it truly is.

Banana and Blueberry Toad in the Hole

SERVES
6-8

Bananas are a wonderfully sweet fruit, but when cooked they become caramelised and have a gentle toffee flavour. That said, this isn't a cloyingly sweet brunch dish; it's just about right and the blueberries add a subtle sourness anyway. The batter is essentially a roasted pancake, so it couldn't be simpler.

---

3 large ripe bananas

50g self-raising flour

---

1 small egg

150ml full-fat milk

100g blueberries

50g unsalted butter

Preheat the oven to 220°C/200°C fan/gas mark 7.

Slice the bananas along the length so you have 6 long halves. Place them into a medium-sized roasting dish (mine is 30cm × 20cm). Cube the butter and scatter it over the bananas, cover them with foil and then roast in the oven for 10 minutes.

Meanwhile, make the batter. Put the flour into a mixing bowl and add the egg and 25ml of the milk. Whisk to a thick, smooth paste, then slowly pour in the remaining milk, whisking constantly.

Once the bananas have had their 10 minutes there will be a little moisture in the dish from the bananas, that's normal. Pour the batter over the bananas, then quickly scatter over the blueberries – I do this while the dish is still in the oven to ensure it stays hot, but don't risk burning yourself. Bake, uncovered, for 25–35 minutes or until the batter has puffed

Variation
In place of the blueberries, raspberries work beautifully. And, rather than buy fresh, frozen berries work just as well and there's no need to defrost them first.

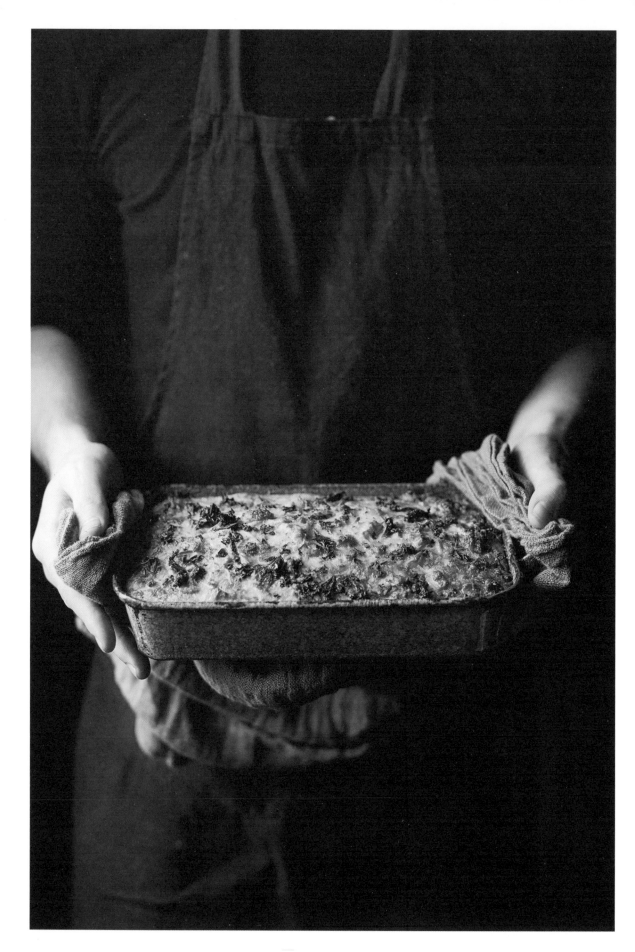

Sausage, Kale and Potato Bake

When I asked around as to what brings people comfort, so many responded with 'carbs and cheese'. It's impossible to deny it: that combination has an instant warming and calming effect.

The added beauty of this is that you can prepare the entire thing a day in advance. Just assemble as detailed, then throw it into the fridge – get it out a good 30 minutes before you bake it, though.

With the sausages, I insist that you get the best quality you can, preferably those with a high mace or nutmeg content to bring an extra something to the dish. I get my sausages from Heap's Sausages in Greenwich, London.

SERVES
4–6

Preheat the oven to 200°C/180°C fan/gas mark 6.

Into a mixing bowl, squeeze the meat out of the sausages and discard the casing. Finely chop the kale – I also remove the thicker stalky bits – and add to the bowl. Heat 1 teaspoon olive oil in a frying pan over a medium–high heat and add the meat and kale. Fry until the meat is cooked and slightly browned, then place into a clean mixing bowl.

Peel the potatoes and coarsely grate them. Place the grated potato onto a clean, dry tea towel or muslin and sprinkle 1 teaspoon salt all over them. Tightly squeeze the potatoes in the cloth to remove every last drop of moisture, then add to the pan, with another teaspoon of oil, and stir-fry until soft.

Add the cooked potatoes to the bowl with the kale and sausage meat. Grate the cheese and add to the bowl. Season with 1 teaspoon black pepper and just a pinch more salt, then toss together until fairly evenly dispersed.

Beat the eggs in another bowl, then add to the potato mixture and stir together. Tip into a pie dish or medium-sized enamel tray and bake in the oven for 40–50 minutes, until golden brown and set. Remove from the oven and allow to cool for 10 minutes before digging in.

500g sausages

150g kale

400g floury potatoes (Maris Piper)

250g strong Cheddar cheese (or Emmental)

9 large eggs

Sea salt flakes
Coarse black pepper
Olive oil, for frying

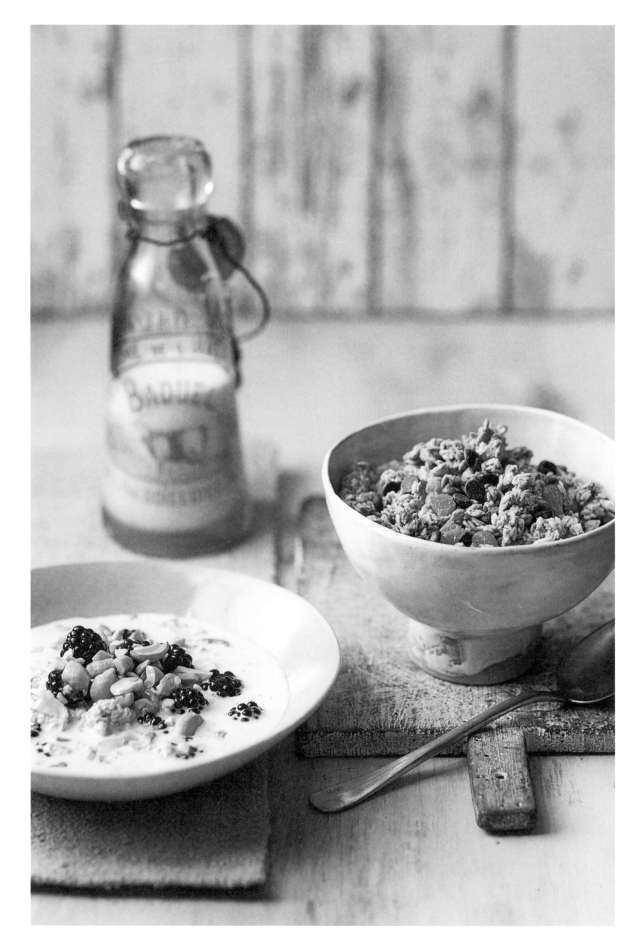

Cashew Nut, Blackberry and Maple Overnight Oats

SERVES
2

This couldn't be simpler: just mix together the oats and milk in a bowl. Cover with cling film and refrigerate overnight.

In the morning, roughly chop the cashew nuts and halve the blackberries – though that could be done the night before, especially if you're one of those late risers who struggles to get ready and out of the door on time. Fold those into the oat mixture with the maple syrup and serve – you can add more milk, if it makes you happy.

Variation
You could swap the blackberries for any berry, and the nuts for any nut – this recipe is so versatile. And, of course, if you don't do dairy, almond or soya milk would work well.

140g rolled oats

475ml milk, plus extra to serve (optional)

50g cashew nuts

170g blackberries

3 tablespoons maple syrup

Peanut Butter and Chocolate Chip Granola

MAKES
8–10
PORTIONS

Preheat the oven to 150°C/130°C fan/gas mark 2.

Place the oats in a large mixing bowl. In a saucepan stir together the maple syrup and peanut butter over a medium heat, until they mix together and become looser. Pour the maple syrup and peanut butter mixture over the oats and stir until all of the oats are covered – the mixture will clump together into little nuggets, and that's exactly what you are looking for.

Scatter the mixture over a large baking sheet – you may need to do this on two baking sheets – and allow to dry out in the oven for 45 minutes, shaking the trays to mix everything up halfway through so that the nuggets colour evenly. Remove from the oven and allow to cool and crisp on the baking sheets.

Chop the apricots into small chunks and toss them into the cooled granola with the chocolate chips and stir through to distribute them evenly. Store in an airtight tub or jar where it will last for a good 5 or 6 weeks.

350g jumbo rolled oats

180g maple syrup

180g crunchy peanut butter

150g dried apricots

100g dark chocolate chips

Nectarines with Thyme, Honey and Strawberry Yoghurt Cobbles

SERVES
2-4

Brunch doesn't have to be piles of pancakes and bacon (though that's never a negative thing), something a little lighter that sets you up for the day can be just as welcome. This – which is essentially a basic cobbler – is simple yet satisfying at the breakfast table.

4 nectarines

5 teaspoons runny honey, plus a little extra to drizzle

3 sprigs of thyme (I use lemon or broad leaf)

100g self-raising flour

130g strawberry-flavoured yoghurt

Sea salt flakes
15g unsalted butter, at room temperature

Preheat the oven to 200°C/180°C fan/gas mark 6.

Slice the nectarines in half, then carefully remove the stones – the best way is to very gently twist the two halves back and forth in opposite directions until loose enough that one half comes free from the stone. Remove the stone from the other half with a teaspoon, gently. Slice each half into four and put into a roasting tray. Spoon over 2 teaspoons of the honey and toss together with the thyme.

For the cobbles, toss the flour in a mixing bowl with the smallest pinch of sea salt. Rub the butter into the flour until evenly dispersed and the flour resembles inelegant yet fine breadcrumbs. Pour the yoghurt and remaining honey into the bowl and stir in – just until well amalgamated; you don't want to overmix this. The mixture should be very thick but scoopable. Leave the dough to rest for 15 minutes, then spoon fairly even tablespoonfuls randomly over the nectarines.

Bake in the oven for 25–30 minutes or until the nectarines are juicy and hot and the cobbles have swollen and are a light golden-brown colour. Serve warm.

Variation
Any soft, stone fruit would work well. Apricots would offer a little more sharpness and so perhaps may need a tad more honey.

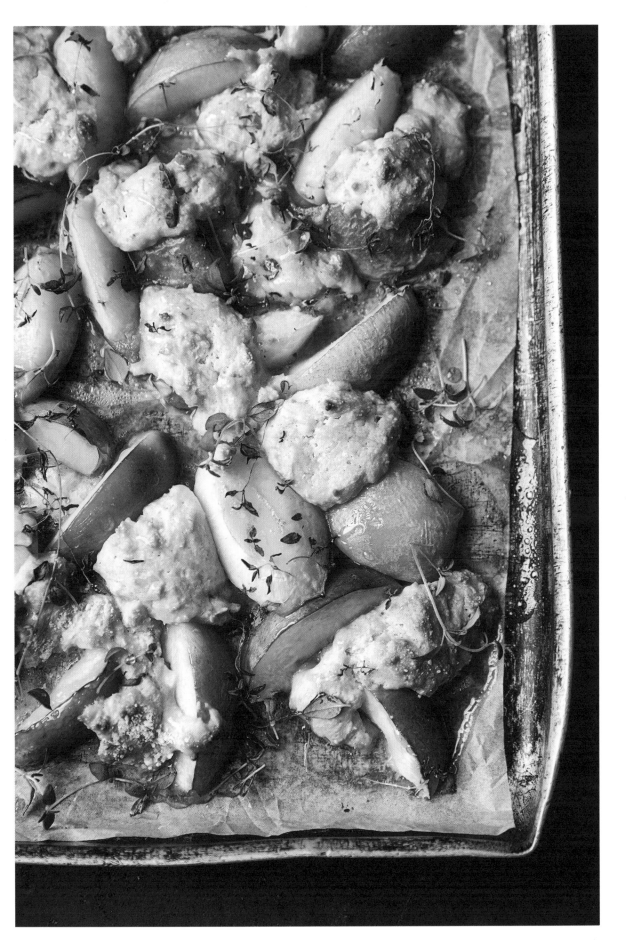

Crashed Breakfast Eggs

SERVES
2

I once ran away to Madrid where I fell in love, though really my love affair was with this dish. I ate it every day for brunch, and I make it so often now. The beauty of it is not only its simplicity, but also that it's a great recipe to experiment with – adding chorizo or pancetta in place of the sausage works particularly well. Traditionally this is made with potatoes, but this version is a little lighter on the carbs.

3 best-quality sausages

2 small bell peppers (I use red and yellow)

4 spring onions

4 large eggs

50g Manchego cheese

Olive oil
Sea salt flakes
Coarse black pepper

Slice the sausages into 1cm chunks. Deseed the peppers and slice them finely, chop the spring onions into 1cm pieces and set aside until needed.

Heat 1 tablespoon olive oil in a frying pan over a high heat. Once the oil is hot, add the sausage chunks, turn the heat down to medium and fry for a good few minutes until cooked through, stirring them often. Add the peppers and spring onions and fry for a minute or so, just until softened.

Hold the eggs about 30cm above the pan and crack them open, allowing the insides to tumble and crash into the pan. Leave the eggs to fry for 2 minutes or so, until they are only just set. Grate the cheese and scatter it on top, then season to taste.

Maple-coated Bacon with Cinnamon Baked Apples

SERVES
4

Pork and apples: two ingredients that just go together without any question. This brunch version of the classic combination is slightly sweeter, and so more palatable when eaten first thing. The Granny Smiths are perfect here: not only are they sharp and so suited to the candied bacon, but also they don't break down as much as other apple varieties when cooked. You're free to use whichever brand and style of bacon you prefer, but with the maple and cream cheese inspiration stemming from America, I feel that American-style smoky bacon is more fitting.

4 Granny Smith apples

½ teaspoon
ground cinnamon

8 rashers
American-style
(smoked streaky) bacon

40ml maple syrup

4 tablespoons full-
fat cream cheese

40g unsalted butter,
at room temperature

Preheat the oven to 200°C/180°C fan/gas mark 6.

Core the apples and slice them in half widthways. Arrange them in a baking tray and sprinkle with the cinnamon. Put a blob of butter onto each apple half.

Have a separate baking sheet ready for the bacon – though if you've got a wire rack that fits onto the baking sheet, use that, as it'll help to get the bacon crispy. Put the rashers into a mixing bowl and rub the maple syrup into them as evenly as possible. Arrange the rashers, well spaced, on the baking sheet or rack and pour over any remaining maple syrup.

Pop everything into the oven and cook for 25 minutes. The apples should soften but retain their shape and the bacon should be crispy – if you like it really crispy, you may wish to leave it in the oven a little longer.

Serve the apples with a blob of cream cheese and topped with the bacon – you can chop it finely or serve it as crispy rashers.

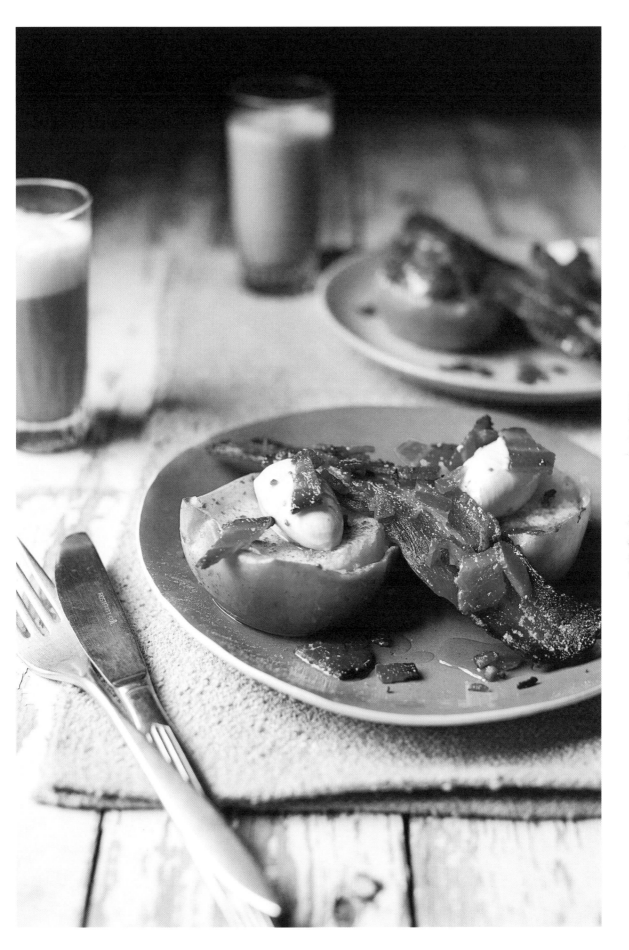

Lady Grey Poached Prunes with Yoghurt and Caramelised Oats

SERVES
4-6

Any fruit poached in syrup is bound to satisfy, but there's something particularly intriguing about the intense, almost molasses sweetness of prunes. The Lady Grey tea has a haunting bergamot-citrus flavour which permeates into the syrup and prunes and is so wonderful atop creamy, thick yoghurt. Do go for the packets of dried prunes as opposed to the syrup-soaked variety; because the former are drier they absorb much more of the poaching liquid.

6 Lady Grey tea bags

190g caster sugar

500g dried prunes

40g rolled oats

500g Greek yoghurt

300ml water

Put the water, tea bags and 150g of the caster sugar into a saucepan and bring to the boil. Reduce to a simmer and cook for 5 minutes, then add the prunes and return to the boil for just 1 minute. Remove from the heat and allow to cool to room temperature. Once cooled, remove and discard the tea bags, then decant the prunes and syrup into a bowl, cover with cling film and leave overnight. If you prefer, you could decant them into a clean jar and store them in the fridge for up to a month.

Heat a dry frying pan over a high heat. Once the pan is hot, add the oats and toss them about in the pan for a minute or so to toast, then sprinkle in the remaining 40g caster sugar. Let the sugar caramelise and coat the oats, then tip out onto a plate and allow to cool. If preparing in advance, store the oats in an airtight container with a slice of bread – the bread will hopefully soak up any humidity before the oats do.

To serve, simply pile the desired amount of prunes and their fruity tea syrup over a blob of yoghurt and top with the caramelised oats.

Rye Soda Bread
with Egg Butter

MAKES
1 LOAF

Whenever I revel in the simplicity of making soda bread, I always feel as though I should crumble with guilt. For me, the idea of breadmaking conjures images of patience, but with soda bread that waiting time is obliterated. This egg butter is to die for. It is common in eastern Finland, western Russia and the bit in the middle: Karelia. And the saltier the butter, the better it is. The egg butter will keep in the fridge for up to a week.

250g wholemeal
rye flour, plus
extra for dusting

2 teaspoons
baking powder

200ml buttermilk,
plus 2 tablespoons

5 large eggs

2 tablespoons dill

180g salted butter,
at room temperature
Sea salt flakes

For the bread, in a mixing bowl toss together the flour, baking powder and 1 teaspoon sea salt. Rub 40g of the butter into the flour until it comes together to form inelegant breadcrumbs. Whisk together 200ml buttermilk and 1 of the eggs, then quickly but carefully mix this into the dry ingredients using a wooden spoon to create a rough, scraggy mass. Once the mixture comes together, sprinkle a little flour onto the worktop, tip out the dough and work it – this isn't as vigorous as a kneading; it's more of a coaxing – until the dough comes together to form a ball. The dough will be fairly wet, so don't work it too much, just roll it into a ball.

Preheat the oven to 200°C/180°C fan/gas mark 6.

Place the dough ball onto a baking sheet lined with baking paper, pat it down lightly into a thick disc and cut a deep cross into it – essentially, cut it into quarters barely attached at the bottom. Leave the loaf to rest at room temperature for just 20 minutes, then bake for 30–35 minutes, until crispy on the outside. This won't puff up anywhere near as much as a plain-flour soda bread, but that's absolutely fine – rye loaves are better that bit denser. Leave to cool on a wire rack.

For the egg butter, bring a medium saucepan of water to the boil. Add the remaining 4 eggs and boil for 8 minutes, then gently tip out the water and place them under cold running water. Once the eggs are cool enough to handle, peel them and chop them finely. Chop the dill finely, too, then mash together the eggs, remaining 140g of butter, 2 tablespoons buttermilk and the dill. To serve, slather the butter onto chunks of the bread.

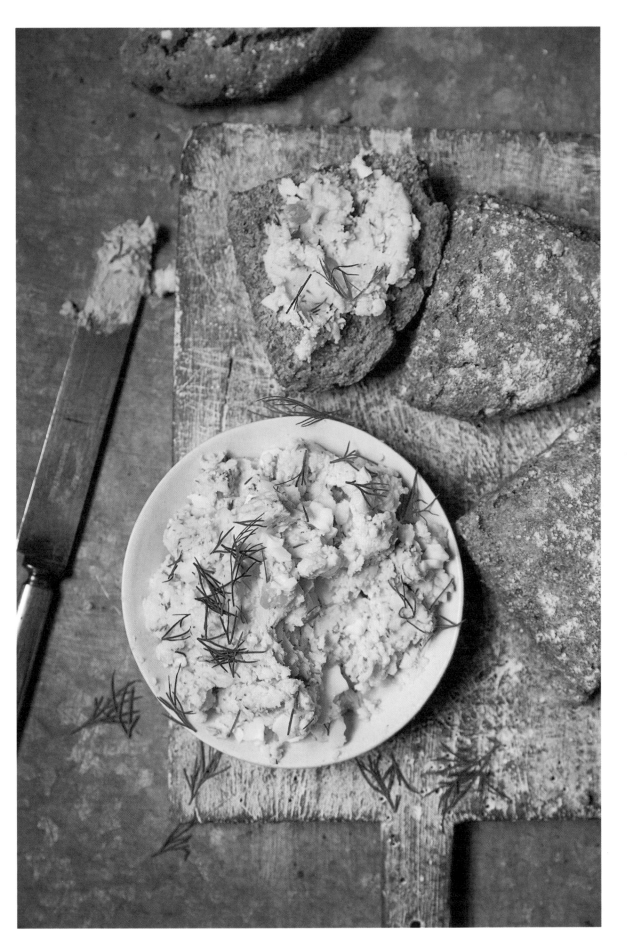

Sweet Potato Hash with Egg, Pancetta and Sage

SERVES
1

We've all done it: had a little too much to drink the night before and woken up craving something savoury, full of carbs and flavour. This really hits the spot. With a wedge of buttered bread or toast on the side, it's worth the hangover. This doesn't need to be reserved solely for those mornings of regret though; it's a fairly balanced dish to kick-start any day.

300g sweet potato

---

1 banana shallot

---

2 sage leaves

80g pancetta or
smoked bacon lardons

---

1 large egg

Sea salt flakes
20g unsalted butter
Coarse black pepper

Bring a medium-sized saucepan of well-salted water to the boil. Meanwhile, peel the sweet potato and chop it into 1cm cubes. Once the water is boiling, add the sweet potato chunks and bring back to the boil. Boil for 5 minutes, then drain.

Finely slice the shallot and set aside. Put the lardons and butter into a frying pan set over a medium heat and cook, stirring occasionally, for a good 5 minutes until the pancetta fat renders down, then add the shallot and allow that to soften.

Add the sweet potato cubes to the frying pan and stir-fry for 1–2 minutes until heated through. Chop the sage finely and stir through, then push the hash to the edge of the pan and crack the egg into the centre. Fry just until the white begins to set then reduce the heat to low and cover with a lid until the egg white is cooked but the yolk is still runny. Remove from the heat, season and savour.

Variation
If you're really hungover, try frying 100g minced beef with the bacon and shallot for an extra hit of flavour. And, of course, you could use regular potatoes – go for Maris Piper.

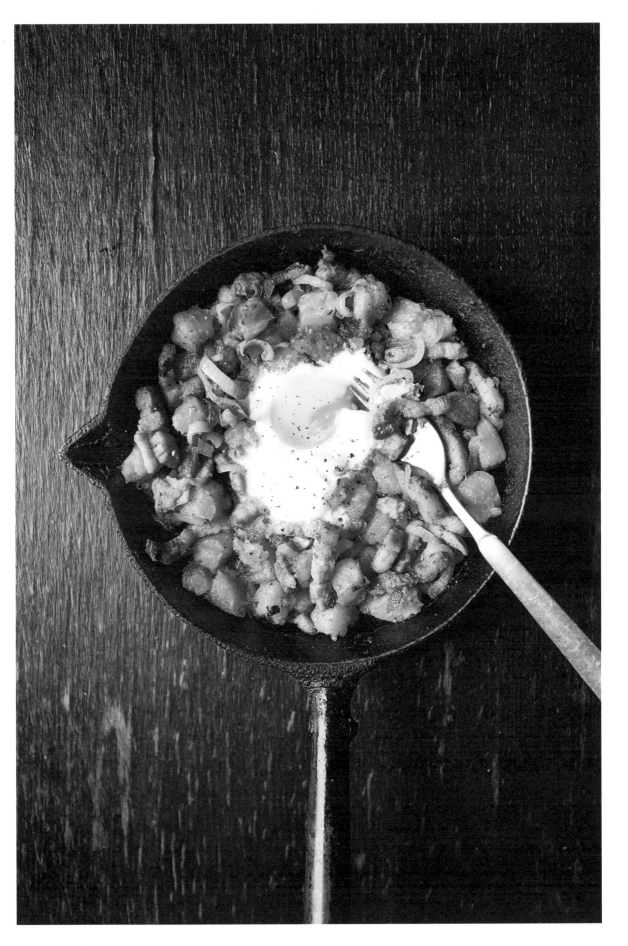

Mushroom Stroganoff on Sourdough Toast

SERVES
1

When it comes to frying mushrooms, I'm an avid believer in Julia Child's method. She says not to overcrowd them in the pan so that they fry rather than steam, so even with the small weight of mushrooms here, it's best to fry them in a few batches so they don't go too soggy. The texture of these fried mushrooms is just right in this spicy, creamy sauce.

200g mixed
mushrooms

1 teaspoon paprika

1 garlic clove

75ml double cream

2 slices of sourdough

40g unsalted butter
Sea salt flakes
Coarse black pepper

If the mushrooms are a little grubby looking, give them a clean: use a clean, slightly damp cloth to wipe away any grit or dirt. Never wash mushrooms, their texture is like sponge and so will soak in any water and become waterlogged.

Melt the butter in a large frying pan over a medium-high heat. Slice the larger mushrooms finely and add one-third of the mushrooms to the butter with a pinch of salt and pepper. Fry the mushrooms, stirring frequently, until they're coloured – a good 5 minutes or more. Repeat with the remaining batches of mushrooms then return all of the cooked mushrooms to the pan.

Add the paprika to the pan, stirring it through for just a minute. Mince the garlic and add that along with the cream, and simmer for a few minutes until the mushrooms are coated in a paprika-flecked, thick sauce.

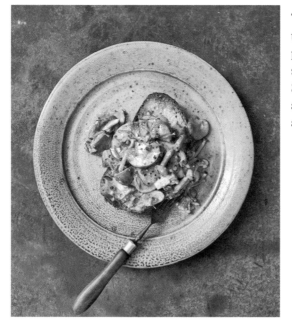

Toast the sourdough until crispy, then pile the mushroom stroganoff on top. Season to taste (I like a lot of pepper here) and serve.

Roasted Plum and Goat's Cheese Bruschetta

MAKES
2 PIECES

It's no secret that a tangy sweet something is the perfect accompaniment to a strong goat's cheese. Add a crunchy wedge of sourdough to that combination and, well, that's pretty much success on a plate. It may seem a little odd to use plums, but actually, when they are roasted with the cinnamon and sugar, they turn into a sort of chunky chutney.

The night before, halve the plums and remove their stones, then slice each half in half – each plum should end up as four slices. Put the slices into a bowl and toss with the sugar and cinnamon. Cover with cling film and set aside at room temperature.

The next morning, preheat the oven to 200°C/180°C fan/gas mark 6. Space the plum pieces on a baking sheet and roast for 20 minutes, or until cooked down and fairly limp.

Meanwhile, heat a griddle pan over a medium heat. Brush the slices of sourdough with a little olive oil. Fry the slices on each side until delicately charred.

Spread the goat's cheese over the charred sourdough and top with a pile of the soft, sweet plums.

4 firm plums

2 tablespoons
caster sugar

1 teaspoon
ground cinnamon

2 slices of sourdough

120g soft
goat's cheese

Olive oil, for frying

Fried Butter Beans
and Avocado

Having neglected to stock up on bacon and eggs before a night out with friends, the next morning we found ourselves ravenous and in need. All I had in were the ingredients for this dish – don't judge me, I'd only just moved in; my cupboards are ordinarily full to bursting.

This gives a somewhat healthier meaning to a 'fried breakfast', but is still such a wholesome morning feast. The butter beans and avocado are both smooth and tender, but when you fry the beans this way, they become ever so slightly crispy on the outside. The trick to getting the most flavour is in slowly cooking the onions so they caramelise and sweeten the dish.

SERVES
2

Peel and halve the onion, then slice it as finely as you can manage. In a frying pan, heat half of the butter over a low heat, and when the butter melts add the sliced onion with a small pinch of salt and 1 teaspoon of the vinegar. Allow the onion to cook down very slowly, stirring occasionally, until mushy but not coloured – about 20 minutes.

Once the onion is cooked, remove it from the pan and put it into a bowl. Drain the butter beans well. Peel and mince the garlic clove and add it to the pan with the beans and remaining butter. Fry over a medium heat, tossing frequently, for 10 minutes, or until the beans are gently coloured and tender.

Chop the avocado in half, remove the stone and then scoop out the flesh and chop it roughly. Add it to the pan along with the onion. Fry for a couple of minutes more, then tip out onto plates. Sprinkle over a little more salt and pepper, if required, then drizzle over the remaining vinegar to taste.

1 medium red onion

400g can butter beans

1 garlic clove

1 ripe Hass avocado

About 4 teaspoons
sherry vinegar

50g unsalted butter
Sea salt flakes
Coarse black pepper

Affogato Monkey Bread

Monkey bread sounds fun, and it most certainly is. It's basically balls of pillowy white bread dough dipped into syrup and coated in sugar, then baked as a whole. Sort of like a very rough and ready share-and-tear loaf. My version – for an exceedingly indulgent brunch – is laced with coffee syrup and served with ice cream, a combination inspired by the Italian classic, affogato.

400g strong
white bread flour

7g fast-action
or instant yeast

180g light brown
muscovado sugar

150ml strong
black coffee

1 litre vanilla
ice cream

Sea salt flakes
130g unsalted butter,
plus extra for greasing
270ml water

Grease a 23cm ring or savarin mould with butter.

I make the dough in my freestanding electric mixer fitted with a dough hook, but it can be made by hand. In a mixing bowl, toss together the flour with 5g salt and the yeast. Add the water – room temperature is fine – along with 50g of the butter. Bring the ingredients together to a scraggy mass, then knead vigorously until elastic and smooth. This will take about 5 minutes on high speed in the mixer, or a good 10 minutes with full-throttle elbow grease by hand.

Bring the dough into a rough ball and place in the mixing bowl. Cover the bowl with cling film, put in a warm place and allow the dough to prove and rise until about doubled in size – up to an hour.

While the dough proves, make the syrup. Place the remaining 80g butter in a saucepan with 80g of the sugar and the black coffee. Stir everything together then bring the contents of the pan to the boil. Boil for just a minute, stirring until well mixed. Remove from the heat and allow to cool a little. Put the remaining 100g sugar into a bowl.

When the dough has risen, gently slap it a couple of times to knock it back – a technical term for 'deflate'. Divide the dough into walnut-sized nuggets – about 30–35 in total. Roll each portion into a rough ball and dunk it into the coffee syrup, then into the sugar. Pile the dough balls into the prepared tin and pour over 2 tablespoons of the syrup, reserving the rest for serving. Allow the dough to rise again, until it comes up to just under the rim of the tin, between 30 minutes and an hour.

Preheat the oven to 180°C/160°C fan/gas mark 4.

Once the dough has risen, bake for 35–40 minutes until puffed up and golden brown. Invert the loaf immediately onto a wire rack and allow to cool for about 15 minutes – you should serve this warm, but not so hot that the ice cream melts instantly. Boil the remaining syrup in a small saucepan until it's thick like honey.

Put the monkey bread onto a serving plate and pile the ice cream into the hole in the centre. Drizzle over the syrup. Allow the eaters to tear off chunks of bread and scoop up lashings of ice cream.

Variation
If you don't have a ring mould you could use a 900g loaf tin instead, and serve slices of the bread topped with scoops of ice cream.

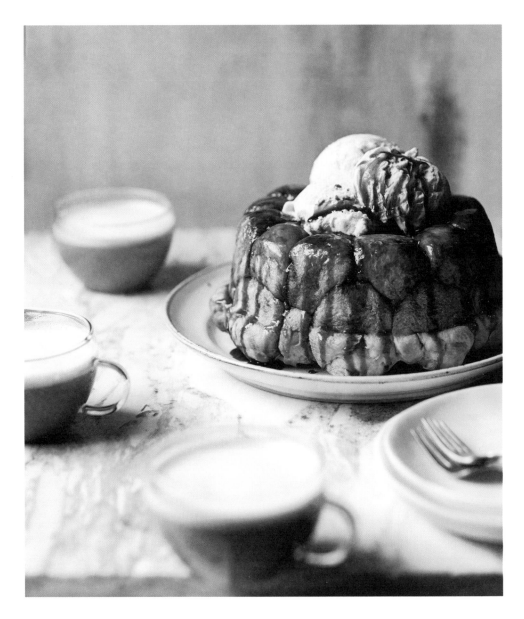

HEARTY PLATES

COMFORT FOODS

We all need comfort. It's part of the human condition to want to silence – or at least mute – the nagging of everyday life. Without wishing for this introduction to read like that of a DIY psychology manual, I feel, as we all do, that it's important to find a moment's peace in our hectic lives.

But comfort is unquestionably a personal thing. Even though we are gifted with empathy, it's impossible to measure those things that bring solace to one person against those of another. You may find a deep cosiness when wrapped in an oversized beach towel as the sun beams down on your toes. That's my idea of hell – sand in my sandwiches infuriates me. You might be most comforted when almost entirely submerged in a stiflingly hot bubble bath – with or without a rubber duck. Or you might just need a few quiet minutes to yourself, staring into blank space.

It's undeniable that for most people, certain foods will act as a consolatory cuddle; the phrase 'comfort food' is internationally known for a reason. I like to think that there are times in every person's life when they need to put down the quinoa and indulge. Even some of the hardiest 'eat-clean' folk I've come by (not that I strive to befriend such austere and ascetic souls) still search for something to enjoy on their 'cheat day'.

Personally, I don't hold with that entire outlook and I don't think anyone should categorise food as clean or unclean. Granted, some foods are richer in nutrients than others, but perhaps what those other foods lack in nutrient density they make up for in reassuring comfort. That may seem like a superficial and convenient notion, but ask yourself this: can you deny that a pie of some form, with rich, flaky puff pastry, brings snuggly warmth? If you can deny that, fair enough, but I sincerely suggest you consciously uncouple yourself from this book and run it through your juicer. I should remind myself here that the pathway to comfort is a subjective one, of course.

It's important to achieve balance without the painstaking guilt that I see so many battle with. My mother says to me, 'you can't have jam on your bread every day'. Perhaps that's a little too frugal, but the metaphor works nonetheless: treats are spontaneous, and that's partly why we enjoy them so much.

The food in this chapter is wholesome, and not just because of the portion sizes or the deeply satisfying ingredients, but because these dishes often play a part in the creation of warm memories, too. Whenever I reflect on a happy time, there's always been some hearty dish involved. Take my Haddock with Braised Chorizo and Leeks, for example: sheltering in my hotel from a bitterly cold winter in New York, I opted for something not too dissimilar. It worked. It brought me instant warmth. I find there are few minor troubles that a bowl of warming broth can't remedy.

Curried Romanesco and Tamarind Soup

SERVES
6-8

Romanesco, the spiky lime-green cousin of the standard cauliflower, is somewhat nuttier than the regular variety. It has such a great flavour and, as with any vegetable, once it is roasted that flavour amplifies. Roasted cauliflower on its own or as a side dish is delicious (see my Mulled Wine Brisket with Roasted Cauliflower on page 111), but when you take that intensified taste and add it to a few other ingredients, you get something so complex and wonderful.

Tamarind is the very tangy fruit from the tamarind tree, which can be processed into either dense blocks or paste. Both are readily available in larger supermarkets (usually on the world or foreign food aisles) and, of course, online.

600g Romanesco cauliflower

1 large red onion

2 tablespoons curry powder

1 litre good-quality chicken or vegetable stock

2 tablespoons tamarind paste

Olive oil, for roasting
Sea salt flakes
Coarse black pepper

Preheat the oven to 220°C/200°C fan/gas mark 7.

Chop the cauliflower into large florets – and don't neglect the stalk, which has so much flavour. Peel the onion and cut it into quarters, leaving the root end intact so the individual layers don't flake apart and burn, though do shave off the thread-like roots with a sharp knife. Place the cauliflower pieces and onion into a roasting tray and add 3 tablespoons of olive oil, the curry powder and 1 teaspoon each of salt and pepper. Toss together so that everything is well coated, then roast for 20–25 minutes, or until the cauliflower just starts to char and the onion is fairly soft.

While the vegetables roast, bring the stock to the boil in a large saucepan, but don't leave it boiling; just get it hot, then remove from the heat. Once the vegetables have cooked, add them to the stock, cover with a lid and simmer for 10 minutes. After this time, remove a ladleful of the cauliflower florets, for decoration, then blitz the rest until smooth – either in batches in a food processor or with a handheld stick blender.

Return the soup to the saucepan and stir in the tamarind paste. Check the seasoning, adding more salt and pepper if necessary, then serve with the reserved florets of cauliflower on top.

As with most soups, this freezes just fine and will keep for a good 6 months in an airtight container, or portioned in ziplock bags. Defrost and reheat thoroughly before serving.

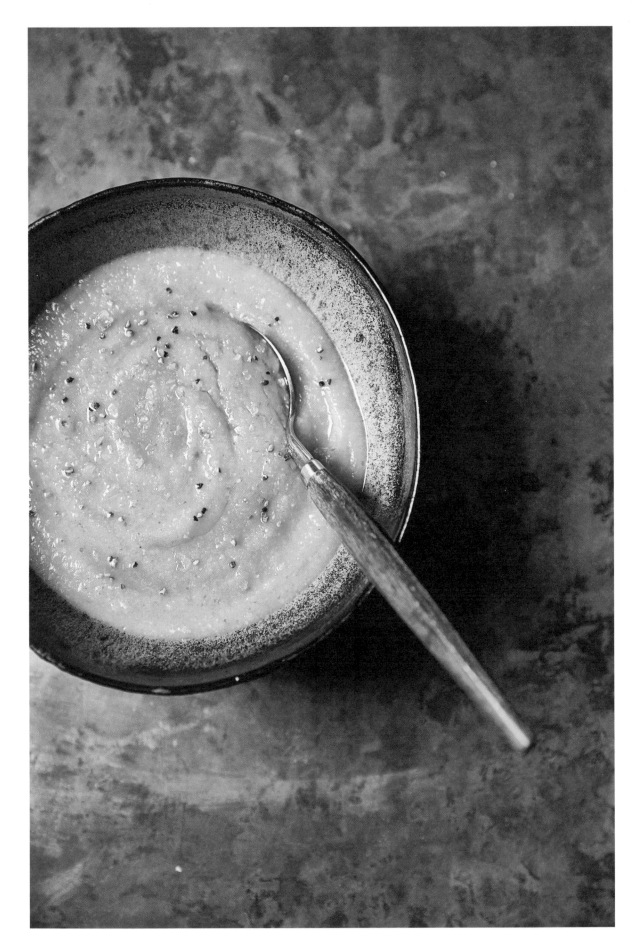

Sweet Potato and Lentil Red Curry Soup

It's as though sweet potatoes and lentils were divinely created especially for soups and curries. They swell and so bulk the dish, but they also absorb flavours: each sip of this soup is spiked with the spiciness from the paste, balanced with the sweetness of the potato. The sharp tang from the lime brings out every element of flavour.

SERVES
6–8

Peel the sweet potatoes and chop them into 1cm cubes. Rinse the lentils in a sieve under cold running water until the water runs clear.

Heat a large saucepan or casserole – one you have a lid for – over a high heat. Add the red curry paste and stir-fry for just 1 minute, until it becomes strongly aromatic. Quickly add the potato and lentils and stir to coat in the paste, then pour in the stock. Bring the contents of the pan to the boil, then reduce to a very gentle simmer and cook with the lid on for 35–40 minutes, just until the lentils and sweet potato are soft.

Ladle the soup into a food processor and blitz until smooth and thick. Return to the pan and add a generous pinch of pepper and a pinch of salt, if required. Add the lime juice and stir in before serving.

As with most soups, this freezes just fine and will keep for a good 6 months in an airtight container, or portioned in ziplock bags. Defrost and reheat thoroughly before serving.

Leftover ingredient
Use leftover red curry paste for the Red Curry Sea Bass with Potato Rosti on page 131.

500g sweet potatoes

350g split red lentils

3 heaped tablespoons red curry paste

1.5 litres good-quality stock (I use beef but it's your choice)

Juice of 2 limes

Coarse black pepper
Sea salt flakes

Garlic, Anchovy and Olive Flatbreads

MAKES
4

During a walk with my dad one spring, we came across a forest floor of wild garlic. The little white flowers floating above a thick sea of green leaves had an aroma that was so intense – somewhere between garlic and chive. With the find, we made these flatbreads.

Because wild garlic is seasonal, and seemingly never sold in supermarkets, this recipe uses normal garlic. It's actually an improvement on the original: it's strong enough to retain its own flavour alongside the boisterous hit from the anchovies, which slightly overwhelmed the wild garlic. The lager is used to make the dough itself mainly for flavour. It brings a gentle, fermented depth to the flatbreads, making them even more savoury and satisfying.

200g self-raising flour, plus extra for dusting

130ml lager

4 anchovies from a jar

8 pitted green olives

4 large garlic cloves

Sea salt flakes
6 tablespoons olive or rapeseed oil
Coarse black pepper

To make the bread, simply mix the flour with 1 teaspoon salt and the lager. Bring together into a rough dough, then knead on the worktop for a few minutes or until smooth. Leave the dough in the bowl and cover with cling film to rest for 15 minutes.

For the topping, roughly chop the anchovies and olives and finely chop the garlic. Add to a saucepan with the oil and sauté over a low heat for 1 minute. Remove from the heat and leave the flavours to infuse into the oil.

Divide the dough equally into four. On a lightly floured worktop, roll out each portion of dough to a circle about 20cm in diameter. Heat a dry frying pan over a high heat and, once it is hot, add the flatbreads, one at a time, and fry for a minute or until the topside becomes slightly bumpy. Flip the flatbread over and fry the other side for a minute or so more. You don't want the flatbreads to be burnt, but there's nothing wrong with a few bits of char. If you're cooking on gas, remove the flatbread from the pan – with kitchen tongs – and place it directly onto the flame for 10 seconds. It should swell up slightly. Remove from the heat and stack the flatbreads onto a plate.

Top each flatbread with the infused oil and serve.

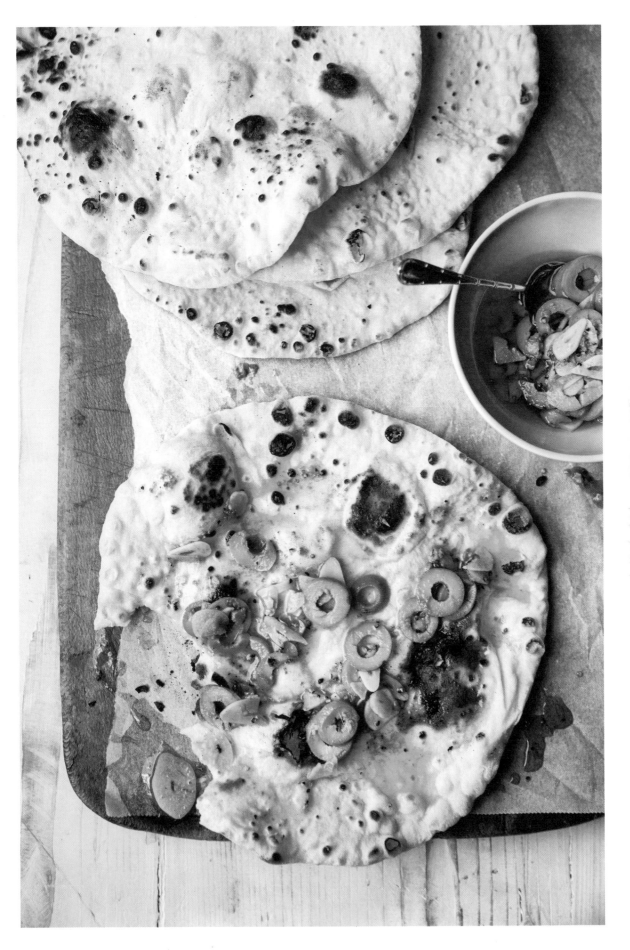

Hummus, Pepper and Dolcelatte Flatbread Pizza

**MAKES
1 LARGE
PIZZA**

This may at first seem a bizarre combination of ingredients, and I suppose it is, but it just works. It's based on the pizzas I used to enjoy at the Grinch wine bar in Manchester. Sadly, it's no longer there, but this pizza perpetuates its memory.

Although the pizza base isn't an authentic one (there's no yeast used), it works very well, but only if the oven is hot enough; the key to any pizza is to ensure the oven is at a ferocious heat. That, and that you have a hot base to slide the raw pizza onto – a pizza stone or a strong baking sheet heated in the oven works perfectly.

175g self-raising flour, plus extra for dusting

2 tablespoons hummus

4 roasted peppers from a jar

100g Dolcelatte

2 teaspoons sweet chilli dipping sauce

Sea salt flakes
150ml water
Olive oil

Preheat the oven to 260°C/240°C fan/gas mark 10, and place a pizza stone or a strong, large baking sheet in the oven to get hot.

Toss together the flour with 3g salt, then add the water and a glug (about 1 tablespoon) of olive oil. Bring together into a dough, and knead for a couple of minutes until smooth. Ball up the dough and leave it in the mixing bowl to soften for 20 minutes, at room temperature.

Once the dough has rested, lightly flour the worktop and roll the dough out into a large, thin circle – if the base is left too thick, it won't crisp up and will stay doughy and soggy. Slide the pizza base onto a well-floured baking sheet. Spread the hummus over the pizza base, then tear the peppers into long strands and scatter them over the top. Crumble on the Dolcelatte, then slide the pizza onto the hot pizza stone or baking sheet and cook for 7–10 minutes, until slightly coloured and very crispy around the edges.

Drizzle the baked pizza with the chilli sauce and serve. You can slice this into neat portions with a pizza wheel, but I like to embrace its flatbread origins and just tear off pieces.

Note
The hummus works so well because it is thick and doesn't make the base soggy. I wouldn't recommend using a tomato sauce for the base unless the sauce is extremely thick.

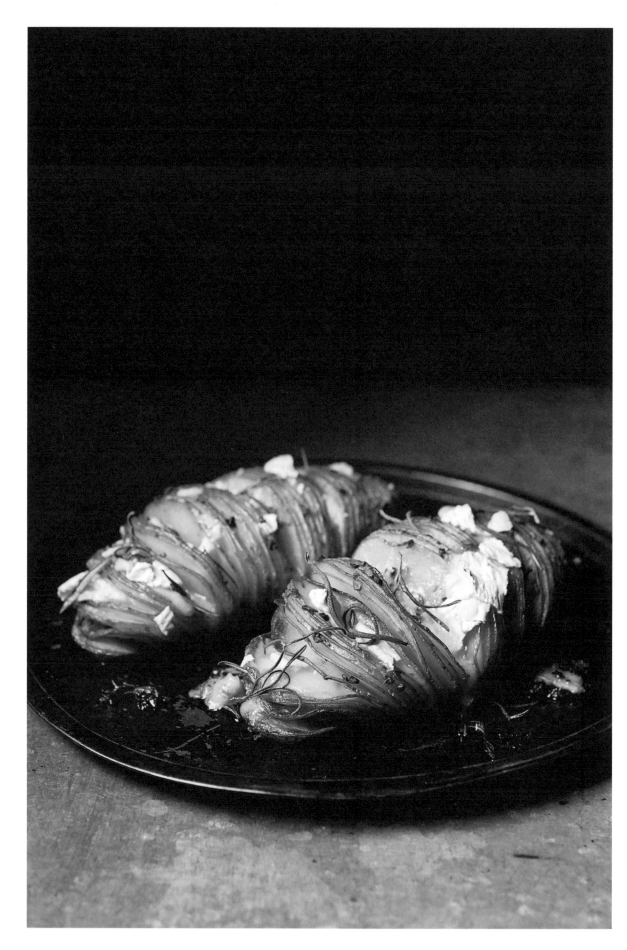

Garlicky, Cheesy, Giant Hasselback Potatoes

There is hardly anything cosier than a baked potato. It's all in the simple perfection of it: crispy, golden skin encasing a fluffy, buttery interior. Whether served with baked beans, cheese or whatever else you prefer, it is a staple – something we may take for granted until the moment we dig in again, when the troubles of the outside world are silenced, even if only for a moment.

This version marries my favourite spud preparation – hasselback potatoes from Sweden – with those buttery beauties that I've relied on for decades.

Preheat the oven to 190°C/170°C fan/gas mark 5.

Clean the potato skins, if necessary, then cut deep slashes into them, but don't cut all the way through. The best way to ensure you don't mess it up is to pop the potato between two wooden spoon handles, and with a sharp knife slice down until the handles prevent you from cutting any deeper.

Finely chop or mince the garlic, and add it to a saucepan with the butter and Worcestershire sauce. Heat over a high heat, stirring, just until the butter melts completely. Pour the melted butter over the potatoes, spreading the slices open as you pour. Bake, uncovered, for 1½–2 hours, until golden brown and crispy.

Remove the potatoes from the oven and tear the Camembert into small chunks, slotting them in the crevices in the potatoes along with the rosemary. Return the spuds to the oven for just 5 minutes, or until the cheese has melted.

MAKES
2

2 large baking potatoes

4 garlic cloves

2 teaspoons Worcestershire sauce

100g Camembert

2 sprigs of rosemary

60g unsalted butter
Sea salt flakes
Coarse black pepper

Sweet Potato, Gruyère and Pecan Gratin

SERVES
4–6

This is a dish that proves you don't always need meat to make a meal. I'm a devout carnivore myself, so you can rest assured that I'm not trying to indoctrinate you with veg-only ways. The nuttiness from the Gruyère and the pecans goes brilliantly with the sweet and earthy potato.

1.2kg sweet potatoes

400ml double cream

Sprig of rosemary

100g Gruyère

50g pecans

Butter, for greasing
Sea salt flakes
Coarse black pepper

Preheat the oven to 200°C/180°C fan/gas mark 6. Grease a 23cm (approx.) pie dish (ceramic is best) with butter. Whatever you do, don't use a dish with a loose bottom or you'll be scrubbing your oven floor for weeks.

Peel the sweet potatoes and slice each very thinly – I use a mandoline or a food processor, but it can be done using a knife, with a straight eye and steady hand. After you've sliced each potato, rearrange the slices as though you were trying to stick them back together to reform the whole potato. Wedge these bundles into the greased dish randomly and at different angles – treat them as though the potatoes were whole, just packing them tightly into the dish.

Heat the cream in a medium saucepan over a low heat. Add the rosemary with a pinch of salt and pepper. Once the cream comes to a simmer, remove from the heat and leave to infuse for 5 minutes.

Pour the infused cream over the waiting sweet potato. Cover the dish with foil and bake for 45 minutes, then remove from the oven and take off the foil.

Coarsely grate the cheese and roughly chop the pecans, then scatter both cheese and nuts over the baked gratin. Return to the oven for a further 15–20 minutes, until the cheese top is bronzed and the sauce is bubbling. Allow to cool and set for 15 minutes before diving in.

Variations
You could try using regular potato with Stilton or Cheddar. If you're not keen on rosemary, exchange it for thyme.

Haddock with Braised Chorizo and Leeks

I adore the somewhat contradictory delicate boldness of smoked fish. A newcomer might suspect that the delicate flesh wouldn't take the flavour, but we all know that it just works. That gentle smokiness pairs so well with the paprika-spiked chorizo. The tender leeks and slightly startling bite from the capers elevate the flavour of this dish – which is essentially a broth – even further.

SERVES 2-4

Preheat the oven to 200°C/180°C fan/gas mark 6.

Cut the chorizo into 5mm slices. Slice the leeks into 1cm discs and place to one side until needed.

Heat a heavy, shallow casserole – one you have a lid for – over a high heat and add the chorizo. Fry the pieces, stirring every few seconds, until the chorizo starts to leak out its orange, spicy oil. Once it does, add the leeks to the pan and fry for 1 minute. Add the stock with a pinch of salt and pepper, bring to the boil, then cover with the lid and cook for 40 minutes in the oven – if you don't have a lid, a piece of foil tightly wrapped around the rim of the pan should be ok.

After 40 minutes, uncover the pan and lay the haddock fillets on top. Return the pan to the oven and cook for a further 10–12 minutes, until the haddock is cooked through. Flake the haddock into the broth beneath, scatter over the capers, check the seasoning – though I find this to be balanced enough – and, finally, serve.

300g raw chorizo sausage

2 large leeks

500ml good-quality chicken stock

2 large smoked haddock fillets (I prefer undyed)

2 tablespoons non-pareil capers

Sea salt flakes
Coarse black pepper

Chorizo and Chickpeas Braised in Cider

SERVES
2

Chubby chickpeas are marvellous. They are surprisingly meaty and have such a smooth, buttery inside. For that reason I'd always opt for the slightly more pricy jarred varieties, as those in cans can sometimes be very tough.

This flavour combination is not new – I had chorizo cooked in cider quite a few times when I spent a summer in Madrid – but it's here to stay. An interesting alternative to cider would be sherry. I've tried it both ways, and loved them both, but I'm a sucker for that sweet sharpness that cider brings.

250g raw chorizo sausage

660g jar cooked garbanzos (chickpeas)

100ml good-quality beef stock

200ml dry cider

Small handful of flat-leaf parsley

Olive or rapeseed oil
Sea salt flakes
Coarse black pepper

In a large sauté pan, heat a good glug of oil over a medium heat. Chop the chorizo sausages into 5mm-thick discs and add them to the pan. Fry the chorizo, stirring occasionally, for about 5 minutes, or until cooked through and just starting to brown.

Add the chickpeas to the pan and stir to coat, then add the stock and cider. Bring to the boil, then reduce to a gentle simmer and cook slowly to reduce, until the liquid in the pan is sparse and thick. Remove from the heat and season to taste.

Roughly chop the parsley and scatter over the top to serve.

Variations
Whilst chickpeas are best for this dish, you could use those gorgeous, plump butter beans from a jar instead.

Taleggio and Salsiccia Mac 'n' Cheese

SERVES
4-6

One of the world's ultimate comfort foods, Mac 'n' Cheese is gooey, rich and fulfilling. Here I've used an Italianate pairing: the fennel-flecked salsiccia sausages, which are so bold in flavour, and the creamy yet tangy Taleggio cheese. The real trickery in this dish, though, is that the traditional béchamel sauce is substituted with evaporated milk, making cosy indulgence an even quicker feat.

6 Italian fennel
salsiccia sausages

350g small pasta
(I use fusilli bucati)

410g can
evaporated milk

400g Taleggio

125g mozzarella

Sea salt flakes
Coarse black pepper

Preheat the oven to 220°C/200°C fan/gas mark 7.

Place the sausages into a medium-sized roasting dish (use the one you plan to cook the finished dish in, so that it keeps the flavours). Once the oven is hot, cook the sausages for 25–30 minutes until gently coloured and cooked through. Remove from the roasting dish and allow to cool – but leave all of those meaty juices in the dish.

Meanwhile, bring a saucepan of water to the boil and add a few generous pinches of salt. Add the pasta and boil for 9 minutes. Drain, leaving the pasta in the sieve until required.

Reduce the oven temperature to 200°C/180°C fan/gas mark 6. Once the sausages are cool enough to handle, slice them into fairly thick chunks.

Using the same pan, bring the evaporated milk to a simmer and add the Taleggio in chunks. Stir the sauce until the cheese melts and everything is smooth. Stir in 1 teaspoon black pepper and a pinch of salt to taste, then add the pasta and sliced sausages, stirring well to coat everything.

Pour the mac 'n' cheese into the roasting dish. Tear over the mozzarella and cook in the oven for 35–40 minutes, until the sauce is bubbling and the mozzarella is molten and burnished.

Variations
If you can't get hold of the Italian salsiccia, go for a good-quality sausage that contains fennel (fresh or seeds). If you can't find Taleggio, use a strong Brie or Camembert instead.

Rice Krispie-coated Chicken Pieces with Stilton Sriracha Sauce

The idea of coating chicken in breakfast cereal may seem fairly childish, but actually the results are so pleasing. And besides, in America they use cornflakes a lot for coating chicken, so I refuse to be embarrassed by this recipe. With the pungent and piquant dip, this is such a comforting treat.

SERVES
4

In a mixing bowl, combine the chicken pieces with 100g of the buttermilk so that each piece is very well coated. Cover with cling film and refrigerate for 1 hour – or leave it overnight if you can, as the chicken will then be incredibly tender.

Add a generous pinch of salt and pepper to the chicken bowl, mixing well, then dredge each piece of chicken through the Rice Krispies until very well coated.

Pour 1cm (depth) of oil into a deep-sided frying or sauté pan and heat over a medium–high heat. Once the oil is hot, add the chicken pieces and fry for a few minutes on each side until golden brown and cooked through. If they darken a little too quickly, your oil is too hot. Place the cooked pieces onto a plate lined with a couple of layers of kitchen paper to drain off the excess grease.

For the sauce, put the remaining buttermilk into a food processor with the Stilton and Sriracha and blitz to a smooth dip.

Allow the chicken pieces to cool just until you can manage to gobble them up without burning your mouth, then serve with the sauce for dipping into.

Alternative cooking option
For a slightly lighter version, try roasting the coated chicken pieces at 200°C/180°C fan/gas mark 6 for 25 minutes; though they'll not be as dark or as crispy.

600g chicken mini breast fillets (or just cut 600g chicken breasts into smaller chunks)

300g buttermilk

150g Rice Krispies cereal

220g Stilton, at room temperature

100g Sriracha chilli sauce

Sea salt flakes
Coarse black pepper
Oil, for frying

Sticky Black
Sesame Chicken

SERVES
4

Let's face it, a big bowl of white rice and sticky sweet chicken can never see us wrong. This dish is certainly comforting, but it is so in an intriguing way. The honey brings the sticky sweetness and the dark soy sauce isn't salty like the lighter version – instead it is treacly and full-bodied. I prefer black sesame seeds here for the dark colour, but you could use whichever you prefer.

50ml dark soy sauce, plus extra to serve (optional)

50g black sesame seeds, plus extra to serve (optional)

125g runny honey

8 skinless chicken thigh fillets

300g basmati rice

Sea salt flakes
Olive oil

Preheat the oven to 200°C/180°C fan/gas mark 6.

Place the soy, sesame seeds and honey into a small saucepan and bring to the boil. Boil for a few minutes until well mixed, then add a pinch of salt and stir through.

Place the chicken thighs into a roasting dish and pour over the sauce. Coat the chicken pieces well, then roast in the oven for 30 minutes, uncovered.

While the chicken roasts, cook the rice. Rinse the rice well in a sieve under cold running water until the water runs clear. Tip the rice into a saucepan and cover with water – you need it to be a good 2cm above the surface of the rice. Add a pinch of salt and 1 tablespoon oil, then bring the pan to the boil. Once it is boiling, reduce the heat to low, cover the pan with a lid and gently cook the rice for 10 minutes. Remove from the heat – don't even think about taking the lid off – and leave to rest for a good 10 minutes more.

Leave the chicken in the roasting dish and pour the sauce into another saucepan. Bring the sauce to the boil and reduce it until it's a little thicker and stickier. Pour it back over the meat, then serve the sticky chicken over the rice, and do feel free to add extra sauce and seeds.

Cosy Roasted Chicken and Green Lentils

SERVES
4

A roast chicken, done properly, is the epitome of comfort food for me. There's nothing I love more than the smell of a bird roasting: a mouthwatering premonition of the bronzed beauty itself, which later comes steaming from the oven.

To capitalise on the chicken's juices, I set the lentils beneath the bird so that every last drop of fat falls down and bastes them, making a flavoursome broth. That's why a roasting dish with one of those elevated racks is necessary here. If you were to just drop the chicken atop the lentils, the underside of the bird would remain pale, and I want every last inch to be golden.

2 leeks

2 celery sticks

200g green lentils

1 roasting chicken
(approx. 1.75kg)

1 head of garlic

900ml boiling water
75g unsalted butter
Sea salt flakes
Coarse black pepper

Preheat the oven to 260°C/240°C fan/gas mark 10.

Finely slice the leeks and celery and place in a roasting tray – one you have a rack for – with the lentils. Toss everything together and add a pinch of salt and pepper. Add 700ml of the boiling water.

Untruss the chicken and discard the giblets – or freeze them, as I do, ready for a rainy day of stock-making. Soften the butter so that it is malleable but not molten. Repeatedly pinch the skin of the chicken breast to loosen it, then at the neck end carefully work your hand between the skin and the breast meat. Once you have loosened the skin, take half of the softened butter and slide it in between the meat and skin on each breast. Spread the remaining butter over the skin of the entire chicken and season with a pinch of salt and pepper. Place the chicken onto the rack, so that it is elevated above the lentils. Halve the garlic and stuff it into the chicken cavity.

Put the tray into the oven and immediately reduce the temperature to 200°C/180°C fan/gas mark 6. Roast for 30 minutes, then add the remaining water to the lentils – if you can do this without taking the tray out of the oven, do so. Roast for 1 hour longer, or until the chicken is golden brown and cooked through – when you slice into the crease at the top of the leg, the juices should run clear; if they don't, roast for a little longer. The lentils will be a little dry-looking on top, but when you stir them, they'll be deliciously tender.

Serve platefuls of the lentils topped with thick slices of the chicken, or you could plonk the whole tray on the table and dig in – though do get in there before anyone else can; it's every man for himself when a roast is involved.

Chicken, Leek and Cider Mug Pot Pies

SERVES
4–6
(depending on
the mug size)

As I write this introduction, I can't help but giggle at my mum's comments about this recipe. When I handed a pie to her, on a blustery autumn day, she dug in and without so much as a thank you said, in her Northern accent, 'Oh love, there's a lot of leek in here.' But that's the point: lots of leeks, because I love them – especially when they are sweetly caramelised and mixed with dry cider.

500g chicken thighs

400g leeks (about 4)

400ml dry cider

100g full-fat
crème fraîche

320g packet ready-
rolled puff pastry

Olive oil, for frying
Sea salt flakes
Coarse black pepper
50g unsalted butter

Chop the chicken into 2cm nuggets. Wash and trim the leeks (if not already prepared) and slice into thin discs.

Heat a fairly large saucepan over a high heat and add a glug of oil. Once the oil is hot, add the chicken pieces with a pinch of salt and pepper and fry until all sides are more or less seared. Remove from the pan and put into a bowl, setting aside until needed.

Put the leeks into the same pan with the butter and another pinch of salt and pepper, and reduce the heat to low. Allow the leeks to caramelise very slowly, stirring occasionally – this will take a good 20 minutes or so. Once the leeks have cooked down, return the chicken to the pan and pour over the cider. Increase the heat to bring the contents of the pan to the boil, then reduce to a simmer and cook, uncovered, for 45 minutes – you want the cider to evaporate just a little. Remove the pan from the heat and allow to cool.

Preheat the oven to 200°C/180°C fan/gas mark 6.

Once the filling has cooled, add the crème fraîche and more salt and pepper to taste, and stir until well mixed. Divide the mixture between 4–6 ovenproof mugs or ramekins.

For the pastry top, unroll the pastry and cut out discs that are just a little bigger than the mugs, and place them over the filling, tucking the excess pastry around the edge of the mug. Bake the pies for 30–35 minutes, until the pastry is golden brown and puffed.

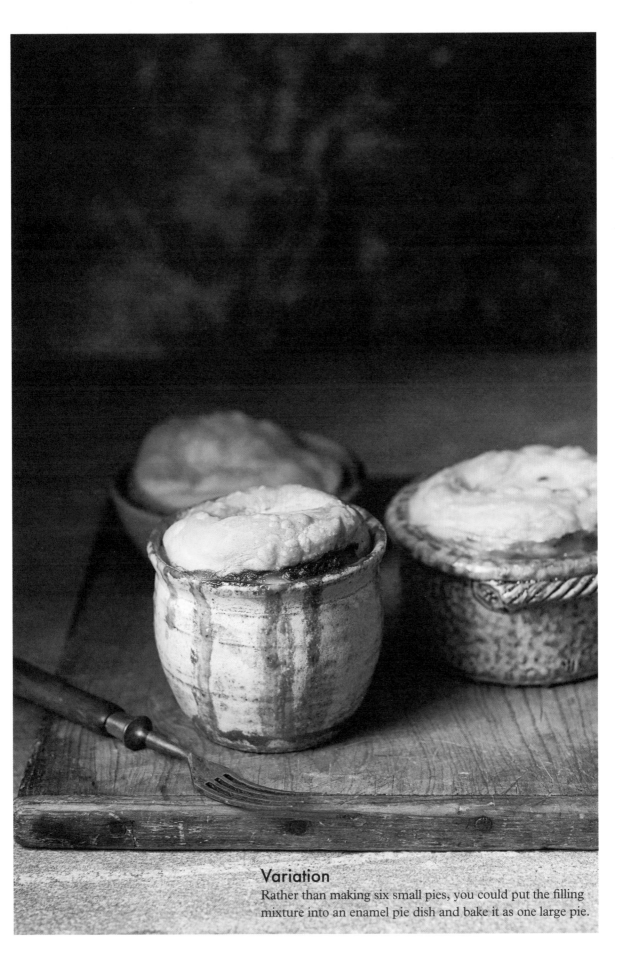

Variation
Rather than making six small pies, you could put the filling mixture into an enamel pie dish and bake it as one large pie.

Eastern Spiced Meatballs with Fiery Tomato Soupy Sauce

SERVES
2

Some like it hot – and I most certainly do. That's something you'll praise or curse me for when you're tucking into this. Obviously, you can reduce the four chillies to just one if you like something milder, but I love how fiery it all is. The addition of butter in the sauce does help to temper the heat somewhat, but the main goal with that is to make it into a velvety, voluptuous sauce – almost like the canned cream of tomato soup I enjoyed as a child.

The meatballs are roasted rather than fried. Not only does that make the whole thing easier but it also ensures the meatballs roast rapidly and so stay succulent.

Preheat the oven to 220°C/200°C fan/gas mark 7.

Quarter the tomatoes and put them, along with the chillies, onto a baking tray – make sure they aren't huddled together otherwise the excess liquid won't evaporate. Sprinkle with a pinch of salt and leave to macerate at room temperature.

For the meatballs, put the minced beef into a mixing bowl and add the spices with ½ teaspoon salt, 1 teaspoon pepper and 3 tablespoons olive oil. Mix everything together until it's paste-like – I use my hands – then divide into 16 portions, rolling each into a compacted ball. Put the meatballs onto another baking tray or roasting tray.

Put the tray of tomatoes and chillies into the oven and roast for 15 minutes, then add the meatballs to the oven and roast everything for a further 10–12 minutes. As soon as the meatballs are cooked through, transfer them to a plate and cover with foil. If the tomatoes don't look slightly charred and limp, leave them in the oven until they do.

For the sauce, remove and discard the stalks from the roasted chillies and put the chillies, along with the tomatoes, into a small food processor (I use my NutriBullet) along with the juices from the meatball pan and the butter. Blitz to a smooth sauce, then serve in bowls with the meatballs studded on top and dusted with a light sprinkling of allspice and cinnamon.

500g vine tomatoes

---

4 fat red chillies

500g minced beef
(at least 15% fat)

---

1 heaped teaspoon
ground allspice, plus
extra for sprinkling

½ teaspoon ground
cinnamon, plus extra
for sprinkling

Sea salt flakes
Coarse black pepper
Olive oil
30g unsalted butter

Cheeseburger Quesadillas

I was, at first, slightly embarrassed by this recipe; it just seemed a little too gratuitous to be included in a cookbook. But after eating my way through an entire batch of these (seriously!) I decided I couldn't leave it out. Especially not from the comfort food chapter: these are too gooey, too toothsome, and they are most certainly too comforting, to be kept as a dirty little secret. And even better, these are doubly indulgent: not only are they stuffed with fried beef and cheese, but the oil from the beef is also used to paint the tortilla before it goes onto the griddle pan.

750g minced beef (at least 15% fat)

4 hot dill pickle cucumbers from a jar

4 white tortillas

400g mature Cheddar cheese

4 tablespoons American yellow mustard, plus extra for dunking

Olive oil
Sea salt flakes
Coarse black pepper

Heat 2 tablespoons oil in a large frying pan over a high heat and, once it is hot, add the minced beef with a generous pinch of salt and plenty of pepper. Stir-fry the beef for a minute or two, until coloured and cooked through. Remove from the heat and put the mince into a bowl – though leave all of the meaty juices in the pan, as these will come in handy.

Heat a dry griddle pan over a medium-low heat. Take a tortilla and place a quarter of the beef over half of the tortilla. Slice a quarter of the pickled cucumber and scatter over the beef, then coarsely grate the cheese and scatter over a quarter of it. Spread 1 tablespoon mustard over the exposed half of tortilla, then fold the tortilla in half, encasing the filling.

Using a pastry brush or your fingertips, paint the uppermost side of the tortilla with the juices from the pan, then flip it into the griddle pan and paint the other side with more juices. Hold the quesadilla down with a spatula for a minute or so until crispy on one side and marked by the pan, then flip it over and cook for a further minute or two – you want the cheese to be absolutely molten and the tortilla to be crispy.

Repeat with the remaining ingredients.

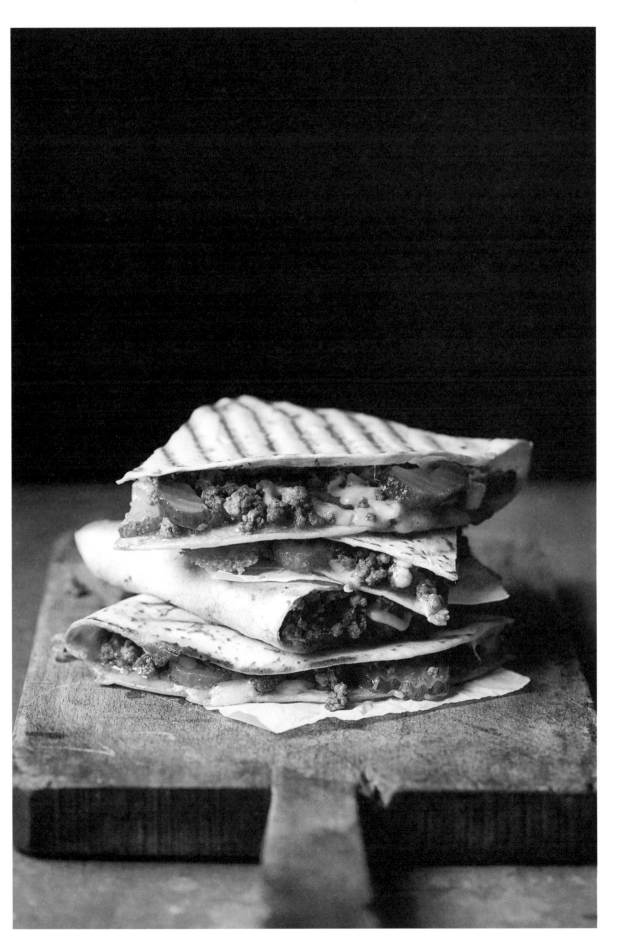

EVERYDAY PLATES

SIMPLE DISHES

Now, what I'm about to tell you might come as a shock, but here goes: you don't need to iron your clothes; your body will iron them for you. It saddens, no, infuriates me, to hear tales of skipping any sort of homemade dinner in favour of a petrol-station sandwich just because there's ironing to be done. And don't get me started on those supermarket-foraged frozen dinners; though, admittedly, there must be a certain stress-relieving quality in the repeated stabbing of a plastic seal. But that is all they're good for, and I'm not falling foul to food snobbery – I just have to draw the line somewhere.

For me, there's no place I'd rather be than in my kitchen, stirring delicious concoctions in pots and pans; though I appreciate that I am lucky enough to do that for a living, so my entire day is spent propping up the hob. That doesn't mean I don't have a stressful job, though, because, believe me, I do, but my oven is my office. And nor do I have the responsibility of child rearing, or having to face a treacherous commute day-in, day-out. I am aware there is life beyond the stove – though I'm not quite ready to accept that yet – so these recipes will slot snugly into a busy lifestyle.

The point I'm trying to make is this: the recipes in this chapter are quick or simple to prepare, and that doesn't mean there will be a sacrifice of flavour or quality. In fact, these dishes didn't originate with time-saving in mind. Some of them aren't so much fast-cooked recipes as faff-free. The primary objective here is that these meals are delicious and fresh, but they just happen to be easy or quick to prepare, too. Serendipity, you may call it.

My initial worry when naming this chapter was that the everyday emphasis might conjure up images of the trite, regimented meals done time and time again. Don't get me wrong, I love a chilli con carne on a Wednesday as much as the next person, but I want to offer something different, something exciting. The meals in this chapter use the regular, everyday staple ingredients (salmon fillets and sausages, etc.), but they're reinvigorated with more rousing, impactful flavours. And don't worry, because these extra, more interesting ingredients are just as readily available.

Roasted Courgettes and Tomatoes with Mozzarella and Basil

SERVES
4

A great benefit to courgettes is how juicy they are. When you roast them, that juice partly evaporates so that not only does the flavour intensify, but it thickens somewhat, too. This makes for an almost self-dressing salad, even more so when paired with the tangy sweet tomatoes. Plum tomatoes, generally, have thicker flesh and less juice, so are perfect here.

400g baby courgettes

225g baby
plum tomatoes

1 small red onion

250g good-quality
mozzarella

12 large basil leaves

Olive oil
Sea salt flakes
Coarse black pepper

Preheat the oven to 220°C/200°C fan/gas mark 7.

Halve the courgettes lenghtways and put them into a roasting tray along with the tomatoes. Add 2 tablespoons olive oil and a pinch of salt and pepper. Peel the onion and cut it into thin wedges, adding those to the tray – the easiest way is to keep the root intact so the layers of each wedge don't fall apart. Toss everything together and roast for 25–30 minutes, until the tomatoes are slightly shrivelled and the courgettes are soft. Allow to cool completely in the tray, then transfer to a serving bowl.

Once the veg has cooled, tear the mozzarella into small nuggets and throw into the veg. Roll up the basil leaves in between your palms, clap your hands together to bruise the basil and release the flavour, then tear it into the salad. Toss everything together, add a little more oil and salt if you feel it necessary, and serve.

Variation
If baby courgettes aren't in season, just use the same weight of regular courgettes and chop them into large chunks – perhaps in half lengthways and then each half into three or four sizeable pieces.

Make in Advance
Because this is served at room temperature, it could be made up to 3 days in advance and kept in the fridge. Though in that case I wouldn't add the basil, extra oil and salt until an hour before serving.

Rustic Mediterranean Tomato Tart

SERVES
8

The vibrant colour of mixed heritage tomatoes is awesome; there is a whole palette to choose from. I particularly love the green tigers, with their verdant skin and dark green stripes and those tiny little yellow ones with a zingy, sharp flavour.

This tart is gorgeous served slightly warm, but I prefer it once it has cooled completely. The flavours just seem to have found one another by the time it has come to room temperature.

320g packet ready-rolled puff pastry

100g soft goat's cheese

400g mixed-colour heritage tomatoes

70g pitted black olives

A few sprigs of thyme

Sea salt flakes
Coarse black pepper
Extra virgin olive oil

Preheat the oven to 200°C/180°C fan/gas mark 6.

Unroll the pastry onto a baking sheet, and with a sharp knife score a 1cm margin around the edge of the pastry – don't cut all the way through, but use enough pressure so that the score line is visible.

Crumble the goat's cheese over the pastry, keeping it within the margin. Slice the tomatoes fairly finely – if you don't have a really sharp chef's knife, a serrated knife is always a good option. Arrange the tomato slices, as higgledy-piggledy as possible, on top of the goat's cheese and sprinkle over a pinch of salt and pepper. Roughly chop the olives and scatter them over the top of the tomatoes along with the thyme.

Bake the tart in the oven for 25–35 minutes, or until the pastry has puffed up around the tomatoes and is a light golden brown. Drizzle over a little extra virgin olive oil and serve.

Variation
Thyme is a personal favourite, but sprigs of fresh oregano are just as beautiful. Tarragon or rosemary are very interesting, but not to everyone's taste – the choice is yours.

Pistachio and Artichoke Panzanella

To hell with low-carb salads, this Tuscan bread salad is where the beauty and flavour lies. Other than its beautiful flavour – a combination that I first tried in Napa, California – I just love how the toasted chunks of bread clatter as they are poured into the bowl; it's a successfully inviting sound.

SERVES
4

Cut the bread into roughly 2cm cubes. Heat a dry frying pan over a medium-high heat and, once it is hot, add the bread and toast for a few minutes. The bread cubes need to be crispy and slightly charred, but certainly not burnt. Put the toasted bread into a mixing bowl.

Add the pistachio kernels to the pan and toss them around for a few minutes, until they smell quite strongly, but don't let them colour. Add the toasted pistachios to the bowl with the bread cubes.

Drain the artichokes, discarding the liquid, and blot them dry with some kitchen paper. Chop the artichokes in half, then fry them for just a minute or two to add colour, before adding to the bowl.

Finely chop most of the parsley – though do save some whole leaves for finishing – and add to the bowl. Toss everything together until well mixed, then tip onto a large serving plate.

To finish, drizzle the balsamic vinegar over the salad along with about 1 tablespoon olive oil. Scatter the reserved parsley leaves on top. Add a pinch of salt and pepper, and your work is done.

200g stale ciabatta or baguette

130g pistachio kernels

240g (drained weight) artichoke hearts from a jar or can

Small handful of flat-leaf parsley

---

2 tablespoons balsamic vinegar

Sea salt flakes
Coarse black pepper
Olive oil

Mushroom and Sage Gnocchi

SERVES
2-4

Once of my favourite midweek treats is a bowlful of gorgeously golden gnocchi nuggets. I have dabbled in making my own gnocchi – I love sweet potato and pumpkin varieties – but the packet version is such a handy weapon in the kitchen armoury, offering almost instant gratification. Ordinarily you boil the gnocchi, similar to pasta, but when fried in butter it becomes crispy on the outside and tender in the middle. To retain that crispness, I don't want the sauce here to be so thin that it makes the gnocchi soggy; it should be intensely flavoured and thick enough to just coat everything.

2 banana shallots

300g mixed mushrooms

About 8 sage leaves

100g dry white wine

400g gnocchi

100g butter
Sea salt flakes
Coarse black pepper
Olive oil

Finely chop the shallots and add them, with 50g of the butter, to a large frying pan set over medium heat. Add a pinch of salt and reduce the heat to medium-low, frying the shallots until softened – a good 15 minutes should do it. Give the pan a stir every once in a while to stop the shallots catching.

Meanwhile, slice the mushrooms thinly and roughly chop half of the sage. When the shallots are softened, increase the heat to high and throw in the mushrooms. Stir-fry them for a couple of minutes until they start to soften, then add the chopped sage and pour in the wine. Allow the wine to bubble and reduce so it coats the mushrooms, but isn't really wet enough to be a sauce. Check the seasoning – you will probably need to add pepper and a touch more salt – then remove from the pan.

Clean the pan and return it to a medium heat, then add the remaining 50g butter. Once the butter melts, add the gnocchi and fry, without stirring or tossing, for 2–3 minutes until golden brown. Then toss about in the pan and fry for a few minutes more. The gnocchi should be slightly crispy so they clatter quietly and invitingly when moved. Return the mushrooms to the pan and stir to coat the gnocchi.

To garnish, heat at least 3 tablespoons oil in a small saucepan and allow it to get hot, then add the remaining 4 sage leaves, frying them for just a minute, maybe less, until crispy. Remove from the pan and blot on a piece of kitchen paper. Serve generous, heaping platefuls of the gnocchi with a crispy sage leaf or two.

Roasted Fine Beans and Chickpeas with Tamarind

Generally, when vegetables are roasted they become sweeter: the natural sugars caramelise and water evaporates, so the flavour is far more concentrated. That's precisely what happens with the beans here, so the natural counterpart would be something tangy and sour. Tamarind is mouth-puckering, and I like it.

Preheat the oven to 220°C/200°C fan/gas mark 7.

Drain the chickpeas and put into a large roasting tray. Trim the beans and put on top of the chickpeas with 1 teaspoon pepper, 1 tablespoon oil and 2 tablespoons of the fish sauce, then toss everything together to coat. Roast in the oven for 25–30 minutes, until the beans have shrivelled and the chickpeas look dry.

Put the roasted beans and chickpeas into a mixing bowl, add the tamarind with the remaining fish sauce and toss to coat. Roughly chop the coriander and scatter over the top before serving.

Leftover ingredient
Use the leftover tamarind paste in my Curried Romanesco and Tamarind Soup on page 36.

400g can chickpeas in water

280g fine green beans

4 tablespoons fish sauce, plus extra for drizzling

4 teaspoons tamarind paste

Small handful of fresh coriander

Coarse black pepper
Olive oil

Lime and Thyme Carrots with Salmon Fillets

SERVES
4

My mother always roasts her carrots in lime juice and thyme, and they are incomparably good. She does that old-fashioned thing of cutting the carrots into angled shards, but I've evolved that and now use baby carrots. I prefer to use the ones with a little bit of stalk intact, but feel free to chop that off if you prefer. When it comes to choosing the juiciest limes, I always give them a good squeeze – they shouldn't be rock solid, but rather should yield a little.

400g baby carrots

4 banana shallots

Juice of 2 limes

4 sprigs of thyme

4 salmon fillets

Sea salt flakes
Coarse black pepper

Preheat the oven to 180°C/160°C fan/gas mark 4.

Place the carrots in a large roasting tray. Peel the shallots and slice them in half lengthways, and add to the tray along with the lime juice, thyme and 1 teaspoon each of salt and pepper. Cover with foil and roast for 1 hour.

While the carrots roast, season the salmon fillets with a pinch of salt and pepper. After the carrots have cooked for 1 hour in the oven, remove the foil and place the salmon fillets into the roasting tray. Return to the oven for 12–15 minutes, until the salmon is cooked through.

Prawn, Mango and Peanut Noodle Salad

SERVES
2–4

Shop-bought, ready-cooked king prawns are such handy little creatures to have in the fridge. Here, with just a few minor preparatory movements, you have a wholesome salad in very little time.

First, rehydrate the noodles: put them into a heatproof bowl and pour over enough boiling water to submerge them entirely. Leave them to soak for 3 minutes, until soft, then drain and allow to cool to room temperature.

Peel and de-stone the mango – the best way is to slice off each cheek, then peel it carefully with a potato peeler. Slice the mango flesh into long, thin slices.

Arrange the noodles on a large plate and top with the prawns and mango slices. Drizzle over the chilli sauce, then roughly chop the peanuts and scatter them over the top. Season if you feel as though it needs it – I personally like a pinch of pepper on this.

150g thin vermicelli rice noodles

1 medium mango

300g cooked king prawns

3 tablespoons hot sweet chilli dipping sauce

75g salted peanuts

Coarse black pepper (optional)

Puttanesca-style Monkfish Stew

SERVES
4

Puttanesca sauce isn't for those with a delicate palate; it is hot, fiery and gutsy. It relies entirely on the brash flavours of salt, chilli and garlic. Traditionally the sauce is made with black olives and salted anchovies. Not wanting to lose either of those vital components, I've opted for anchovy-stuffed green olives – they seem to be much more easy to come by than black, but if you do see anchovy-stuffed black olives, use those.

2 fat red chillies

100g anchovy-stuffed green olives

5 garlic cloves

400g can chopped tomatoes

8 x 150g monkfish fillets

Sea salt flakes
Coarse black pepper
Olive oil

Roughly chop the chillies – I don't bother to deseed them – half of the olives and all of the garlic, then add to a pestle and mortar and grind to a rough paste with 1 teaspoon each of salt and pepper. You could also pulse this in a small food processor, if you prefer.

In a deep-sided frying pan or casserole – one you have a lid for – heat 3 tablespoons of olive oil over a high heat and, once it is hot, add the paste. Stir the paste constantly for a good minute until it has a strong aroma – don't let it catch and burn on the pan. Once the paste is fragrant, add the tomatoes and bring to a bubble. Reduce to a simmer and lay the monkfish fillets on top. Chop the remaining olives and scatter them over the fish, then pop on a lid and simmer gently for 10 minutes, or until the fish is almost completely cooked through and tender.

Remove from the heat, pop the lid on and allow to steam for a few minutes before serving.

Variation
Monkfish works well because it is so meaty and can easily hold its own against that bold sauce. If you need to use a different fish, make sure you choose a meaty white one – hake, pollock or cod would be ideal.

Dilly Devilish Garlic Prawns

SERVES
2

When you eat with your hands (which you absolutely must here), there's something gratifying about a spicy oiliness that coats your fingers and face. And if eaten in a romantic setting, the muckiness helps to break down that initial awkwardness; there's nothing sexier than someone who both loves and lives to eat.

3 fat red chillies

6 large garlic cloves

500g raw jumbo king prawns, shells on

60ml vodka

Small handful of dill

Olive oil
Sea salt flakes
Coarse black pepper

Finely slice the chillies – I don't bother to deseed – and garlic and keep them separate. Heat 75ml olive oil in a frying pan over a medium-high heat and, once it is hot, add just the chillies and stir-fry for about 30 seconds to infuse the oil. Add the prawns with the garlic and fry for about 1 minute. Flip the prawns over and add the vodka to the pan, along with a pinch of salt and pepper. Fry for another minute – the ghostly grey of the prawns should become a warm, pinkish coral.

Roughly chop the dill and scatter it over the prawns. You could serve this in the pan, though the prawns may continue to cook in the residual heat and become a little tough, so it's probably best to tip out onto a serving plate.

Lemongrass and Chilli Clam Broth

SERVES
2-4

When I'm feeling a little under the weather, or simply downtrodden, I'll crave a bowlful of broth spiced with lemongrass, chilli and coriander. Recently I was given some clams and decided to merge my cold-curing broth – which was already made and in the fridge – with my prize. It works beautifully, and is such a quick dish to rustle up.

1kg live clams

3 lemongrass stalks

4 fat red chillies

Small handful of fresh coriander

1 litre good-quality chicken stock

50g unsalted butter
Coarse black pepper
Sea salt flakes (optional)

Put the clams into a colander and rinse under cold running water for a minute. Give the clams a shake and discard any that don't close when tapped on the worktop.

With the back of a knife, bash the lemongrass stalks repeatedly to release all the flavourful oils, and then slice them in half. Slice each half into four, lengthways, to give thin shards of lemongrass. Slice the chillies in half lengthways – you can remove the stalk if you wish, but I don't bother. Separate the leaves from the coriander stalks, placing them in a bowl to one side. Roughly chop the coriander stalks and have them handy with the lemongrass and chilli.

In a heavy-based casserole or large saucepan – one you have a lid for – heat the butter over a high heat and, once the butter melts, throw in the lemongrass, chilli and chopped coriander stalks. Stir-fry for just 1 minute, then add the stock. Bring to the boil, reduce to a gentle simmer and pop on the lid. Cook for 20 minutes to infuse the stock with all of the glorious aromatics. Test the seasoning, adding plenty of pepper, and salt if necessary.

Return the pan to the boil and add the clams. Put on the lid and cook for a final 5 minutes, then remove from the heat. Scatter over the reserved coriander leaves and serve. Don't eat any clams that don't open during the cooking process.

Tahini and Honey Chicken and Paprika Potatoes

SERVES
4

In Paris, on Rue Mouffetard, there is a small stand from which chicken and potatoes are sold. The chicken is slowly cooked on a rotisserie and the fat weeps down onto the potatoes, basting them as they cook. Served in a white foil bag, it makes for the ultimate Parisian lunch, devoured from a park bench.

That experience inspired this dish in a way, only here I've added some of my favourite Middle Eastern flavours. The mix of tahini and honey is really superb, and crisps up beautifully on the chicken.

Preheat the oven to 210°C/190°C fan/gas mark 7.

In a large bowl, mix together the tahini and honey with 1 teaspoon each of salt and pepper. Remove the skin from the chicken drumsticks and slash each one three times. Add the drumsticks to the marinade and coat them well. Refrigerate until you are ready to roast.

Slice the potatoes in half, though leave any particularly tiny ones whole, and tip into a large roasting tray. Add 1 tablespoon olive oil, a pinch of salt and pepper and the paprika, toss together until the potatoes are well coated and roast for 20 minutes.

After this time, lay the drumsticks on top of the potatoes and roast for a further 25–30 minutes, until the chicken is cooked through and the marinade is crispy.

150g tahini

80g runny honey

8 chicken drumsticks

About 24 small
new potatoes

1 tablespoon paprika

Sea salt flakes
Coarse black pepper
Olive or rapeseed oil

Roasted Sausage and Apple with Sauerkraut

A midweek sausage supper is reassuringly simple and, even better, it doesn't skimp on flavour or the general feeling of being satisfied. The best-quality sausages are always a must: I'd opt for the supermarket's best own brand or those from an excellent butcher. And, of course, you can quite easily, and absolutely should, customise this dish with different flavours of sausage – a fiery, chilli-flecked banger would do just the trick for me.

Preheat the oven to 200°C/180°C fan/gas mark 6.

Put the sausages into a roasting tray and drizzle with a little olive oil. Cut the apples into quarters – I don't bother to core or peel them. Slice the onion in half through the root, leaving the root intact, and peel it. Cut it into eight wedges and arrange these, with the apples, in the roasting tray. Top with the thyme sprigs and season with a pinch of salt and pepper.

Roast in the oven for 30–40 minutes, until the sausages are bronzed and the apples and onion are quite softened. You can turn the sausages midway through, if you prefer a more even colouring; though I'm not particularly concerned. Scatter over the sauerkraut just before serving.

8 good-quality sausages

2 Granny Smith apples

1 large onion

A few sprigs of thyme

2 tablespoons sauerkraut

Olive oil
Sea salt flakes
Coarse black pepper

Leftover ingredient

The sauerkraut will keep for a while in the fridge. It's gorgeous in ham sandwiches, stirred into soups, scattered over pizzas or stews. It brings its flavour-boosting qualities to any dish, really, but it's delicious in its own right, too.

Harissa Minute Steak Kebabs

SERVES
4

Harissa is one of the things I always have in the cupboard in abundant supply. It is warming and spicy, yet ever so slightly tangy, and goes perfectly with pretty much anything – I've been known to toss together flaked mackerel with harissa and pasta as a lazy, last-minute lunch. I particularly love the deep red-pepper paste here on the minute steaks: because the steaks are so thin, you can rest assured that with every bite you'll get oodles of spicy flavour.

600g minute steaks

120g harissa

4 flatbreads

4 tablespoons hummus
(I like red pepper
hummus here)

Jar of pickled
green chillies

Sea salt flakes
Coarse black pepper
Olive oil

Mix together the steaks, harissa and a pinch of salt and pepper in a mixing bowl. Cover with cling film and allow to marinate at room temperature for 30 minutes. You could even do this in the morning before you head out, and just refrigerate until needed.

Place a frying pan over a medium–high heat and, once it is hot, fry the steaks for about 45 seconds per side. Remove the steaks from the heat and onto a plate, covering them with foil.

Warm the flatbreads in the pan for just a few seconds per side, then spread each with hummus. Slice the minute steaks into small strips and scatter over the hummus, then add the chillies – as many as folk may fancy. Be sure to drizzle any steak juices left on the plate over the top before serving.

Orange and Sumac Flat Iron Steak with Aubergine and Artichoke

SERVES
4

Although steak, chips and Béarnaise sauce is a difficult combination to compete with, this is a gorgeous alternative recipe for steak. The orange not only offers a refreshing tang, but its acidity helps to tenderise the steaks, too. Sumac is a deep red spice with a sharp, citrus flavour and is absolutely gorgeous with most meats.

The steaks are turned frequently during frying, and that's because with flat iron, as with skirt and flank, the fibrous steak is very easily overcooked and can become tough. This method ensures an even, gentle cooking.

2 oranges

2 tablespoons sumac

4 x 150g flat
iron steaks

2 aubergines

400g (ish) jar or can
artichoke hearts

Olive or rapeseed oil
Sea salt flakes
Coarse black pepper

To make the marinade, simply combine the zest and juice of 1 of the oranges with half of the sumac and 1 tablespoon oil. Rub this into the steaks, wrap them in cling film and leave to marinate at room temperature for 1 hour.

Season the steaks with salt and pepper, then fry each in a hot frying pan for 6 minutes, turning them every minute. If you prefer the steaks a little less rare, fry as above for 8 minutes. After this time, wrap the steaks in foil and allow to rest for a good 10 minutes.

Dice the aubergines into 2.5cm chunks and halve the artichoke hearts. Drench the aubergines in 2 tablespoons oil and a good pinch of salt and pepper. Heat a frying pan over a high heat and, once it is hot, add the aubergine and stir-fry for about 5 minutes, until slightly coloured. Drain the artichokes, and fry them for 1 minute. Place onto plates. Peel and slice the remaining orange and add to the plates, then sprinkle over the remaining sumac.

Slice the steaks into thin strips – do this against the grain of the meat to ensure you get tender pieces – and set on top of the aubergine and artichoke salad. Pour any juices from the foil over the top and serve.

WORTH-THE-WAIT PLATES

SLOW COOKED

There's a smug reassurance in knowing you've got something slowly cooking at home, piping hot and ready for when you return. Whether you're stressed out at work or traipsing around in the cold, when your mind flicks back to that warm stew all stresses seem trivial – if only for a split second. And on returning to the kitchen you're greeted with the ravishing aroma of whatever has been quietly and confidently doing its thing all day. The ultimate welcome home.

I suppose, for that reason, this could be a sub-chapter within the comfort food part of this book: there's no denying that slow-cooked meals have a cockle-warming cosiness to them. But equally, some of these recipes could have slotted into the everyday plates chapter, because cooking like this requires very little attention or effort. It's just a matter of getting the ingredients prepared, then letting them cook away. That's not to say that slow cooking involves no thought whatsoever; it absolutely does. It's important to think about how the meat will cook: if the particular cut is diced too small it leaves a greater surface area to meat ratio, so there's a risk of the meat drying out all too quickly. But there's little need to worry about all that here because in these recipes I've done the working out for you.

So these recipes are worthy, I feel, of a chapter of their very own. This is a slow-cooked chapter, but it isn't a slow cooker chapter; I do all of my slow cooking in the oven. Environmentalists may harp, but it's not a decision I've made without due consideration. If the main reason for buying a slow cooker is to reduce electricity consumption, that is fair enough – slow cookers use far less energy than a domestic electric oven. In my constant pursuit of flavour, though, I find that slow cookers never seem to do the job quite properly. The results, for me, are often too watery or insipid; the oven seems to force the flavours to merge and mingle. But you might think my fear is ill-founded, so feel free to use whichever method suits you best; just make sure that if you do use a slow cooker, follow the manufacturer's instructions with my method in mind.

That being said, whichever you choose, it's impossible for me to be too prescriptive about timings. As soon as the meat flakes apart when pronged with a fork, take it away from its heat source. This inaccuracy is down to so many variables: while modern ovens are reasonably reliable, there could still be some discrepancy. The pot in which the food is cooked also has an unbelievable impact: too thin a material and the dish could quickly overheat. For the avoidance of doubt, any recipes which are cooked in a 'casserole' or 'heavy-based saucepan', I use a Le Creuset 24cm cast-iron casserole for.

One of the best things about slow cooking is how the fatty, collagen-rich meats can be cooked until they're mouthwateringly tender – fat is life's lubrication as far as I'm concerned. If, for some reason (I'll withhold judgement here), you want to reduce the amount of fat in the dish, I'd recommend you leave it overnight in the fridge before serving the next day. That way, the fat will solidify at the surface and you can easily scoop it off. I don't bother to remove the fat, but I do believe that chilling the food overnight improves the flavour and the texture of the meat anyway, so it's a practice I always undertake.

Four-hour Tomato Pasta Sauce

SERVES
4

You might think life is too short to peel tomatoes, then slowly cook them down into a sauce. And admittedly (I'm not trying to put you off, I promise) you don't get much yield for the amount of tomatoes you buy. But as soon as you taste this sauce you are reassured that it was all totally worthwhile. You may believe you've already had the best pasta sauce possible, but so often it will in fact have been too acidic and watery – the result of using canned tomatoes. Fresh plum tomatoes are best in a sauce like this as they are far fleshier than regular salad tomatoes.

1.5kg fresh
plum tomatoes

---

1 large red onion

---

3 garlic cloves

120ml Italian
Malbec wine

400g pasta
(linguine or tagliolini)

40g unsalted butter
Sea salt flakes
Coarse black pepper
Extra virgin olive oil

Preheat the oven to 160°C/140°C fan/gas mark 3.

To peel the tomatoes, place them in a large heatproof mixing bowl – I do this in two batches – then cover them with boiling water. Leave the tomatoes for a minute or two, then drain off the water and plunge them into cold water. Once they are cool enough to handle, remove the skin; it should hopefully slip right off, but if it doesn't, just pull it carefully. Chop the tomatoes roughly, then set aside.

In a casserole or heavy-based saucepan – one you have a lid for – melt the butter over a medium heat. Finely chop the onion and add to the melted butter with a pinch of salt, and once it starts to sizzle, reduce the heat to low and cook down, stirring frequently, for 20 minutes until mushy but reasonably uncoloured. Peel the garlic and throw the whole cloves into the pan along with the tomatoes and a pinch of pepper. Add the wine and bring to the boil, then cover with a lid and cook in the oven for 3½–4 hours. Do check it after 3 hours, and if it's looking a little dry, add a splash of water.

Once the sauce is ready, check the seasoning and add more salt and pepper if required – I like a lot of pepper here, at least 1 teaspoon, but the choice is yours. Cook the pasta according to the packet instructions, but make sure you put a very generous pinch of salt into the cooking water before adding the pasta.

To serve, stir the pasta through the sauce to coat each strand, then pile, casually, onto plates.

Preserved Lemon and Cider Pork with Couscous

SERVES
4-6

The idea of slow cooking may conjure up images of wintery stews and warming hunks of braised meats, but this method can be a summery pursuit, too. I suppose it's all down to what you throw into the pot. The pear cider here is crisp and sweet and so it marries well with the pork. The preserved lemon gives a little extra sharpness, which perfectly complements the otherwise bland couscous.

1.5kg shoulder of pork

1.2 litres pear cider

6 preserved lemons

8 sprigs of thyme, plus extra for the couscous

400g couscous

Sea salt flakes
Olive oil
Coarse black pepper

Preheat the oven to 160°C/140°C fan/gas mark 3. If it hasn't already been done, remove the crackling skin and fat from the pork and place it onto a baking sheet. Deeply score a few times, rub a little salt into both sides, then set aside.

Heat a heavy-based saucepan or casserole over a high heat and add 1 tablespoon oil. Once the oil shimmers, add the pork shoulder to the pan and sear for about 3 minutes, turning occasionally to ensure all of the flesh is seared. Add the cider, 4 of the whole preserved lemons, the thyme sprigs and a pinch of salt and pepper. Bring to the boil then cover with a lid and put into the oven with the tray of crackling – you'll probably need to use two shelves. Allow to cook slowly for about 4 hours, until the crackling is incredibly crisp and the pork meat is falling apart.

After this time, take everything out of the oven. Remove the crackling from the tray and allow to cool and crisp on a plate. Remove the pork from the pan and put it onto a plate, covering it with foil.

Put the couscous into a heatproof bowl and place the pan of cooking liquor over a high heat and bring to the boil. Once it is boiling, pour enough of the liquid over the couscous to cover by 2cm – you may need to top up with boiling water. Cover the bowl with a plate or cling film, and leave to soak for 10 minutes or so. Fluff up the couscous with a fork and season to taste, adding a small handful of chopped thyme leaves and the remaining preserved lemons, roughly chopped. Shred the pork and serve it on a mound of couscous, topped with some crispy pieces of crackling.

Grapefruit Marmalade Pork Belly with Caramelised Red Cabbage

I adore pork belly, it's one of my favourite cuts of pork. But because it is fatty, it needs to be cooked fairly slowly, and it should be served with something quite sharp to cut through it all.

SERVES
4

The day before cooking, cut the pork belly in half and place it in a resealable food bag. In a mixing bowl, dissolve 4 tablespoons salt in 1 litre of the water, then stir in 1 tablespoon pepper, pour it all into the bag with the pork and seal. Refrigerate overnight or for at least 8 hours.

Preheat the oven to 240°C/220°C fan/gas mark 9. Place the pork slices, out of their brine, skin-side up in a deep roasting dish and roast, uncovered, for just 30 minutes.

Meanwhile, mix together the remaining water and the marmalade with ½ teaspoon salt and 1 teaspoon pepper.

Take the pork from the oven, reduce the temperature to 160°C/140°C fan/gas mark 3, then pour the marmalade mixture over the pork slices and cover the roasting dish with foil. Return the pork to the oven and cook for a further 2 hours, until the meat is incredibly tender. Increase the heat of the oven to 240°C/220°C fan/gas mark 9 and remove the foil. Cook for a final 10–15 minutes. Remove from the oven to rest.

Meanwhile, thinly shred the cabbage. Heat the butter in a frying pan over a high heat then add the cabbage and turn the heat down to medium-high. Stir-fry for 5 minutes, then add the sugar and vinegar and cook, on a low heat, for 15 minutes until soft and caramelised.

Remove the pork from the cooking juices and cut each piece in half. Skim the excess fat from the cooking juices and discard, then serve the cabbage with the pork and a drizzle of the juices.

1.5kg piece boneless and rindless pork belly

6 tablespoons grapefruit marmalade

1 small red cabbage

2 tablespoons light brown muscovado sugar

2 tablespoons cider vinegar

Sea salt flakes
Coarse black pepper
1.2 litres water
30g unsalted butter

Pork Osso Buco with Turnips, Anise and Orange

SERVES
4

The Italian 'osso buco' just means 'bone with a hole' (which refers to the cross-cut of the shank bone), but has become the name for the classic Milanese dish of veal shanks, wine and vegetables. I stumbled across pork hock osso buco in a local supermarket and I yelped with excitement.

Somehow it is the turnips that make this dish so successful. The other flavours are vital, too, of course – I wouldn't dream of discounting the exotic combination of anise and shaoxing – but that familiar pepperiness of the turnips is what I love so much about this. It's like a reassuring phone call home during a long-distance holiday.

1.5kg pork osso buco
(about 8 pieces)

300g turnips

120ml shaoxing wine

4 star anise

2 unwaxed oranges

Sea salt flakes
Olive oil
Coarse black pepper
400ml water

Preheat the oven to 180°C/160°C fan/gas mark 4.

In a large saucepan or flameproof casserole – one you have a lid for – heat 1 tablespoon olive oil over a high heat. Season the osso buco pieces with a pinch of salt and pepper, then fry until golden brown and seared – this is best done in batches. While the meat sears (though do toss it about the pan frequently), peel the turnips and cut into 1cm dice.

Once all the meat is seared, add the turnips to the pan along with the shaoxing and allow the liquid to come to the boil, then return the meat to the pan with the star anise, the juice and thinly pared peel of 1 of the oranges and the water. Put on the lid and cook for 2½ hours in the oven – the meat should be so tender that it is starting to fall from the bone.

Remove the pork and turnips with a slotted spoon, then bring the cooking liquor back to the boil on the stove. Boil until reduced by half, then return everything back to the pan to coat. Peel, segment and roughly chop the remaining orange and add to the stew before serving.

Variation
If you can't for the life of you get hold of osso buco, use an unrolled pork shoulder, trimmed of its fat. In that case, you could cook the crackling as in the recipe on page 98. It would need a longer cooking time – 4 hours should do it.

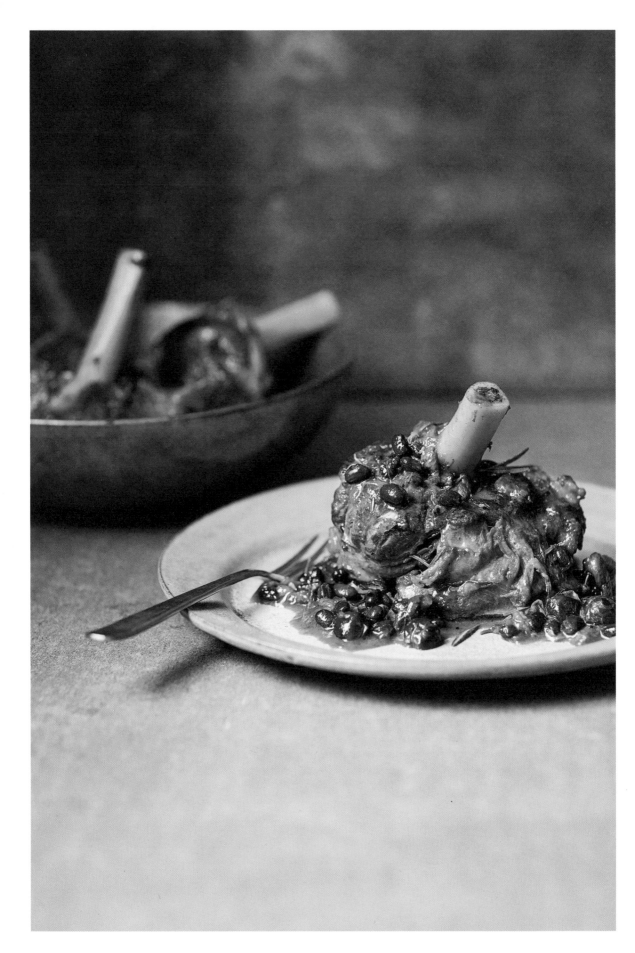

Black Grape Lamb Shanks

When experimenting with this recipe, I was thrilled to discover that the grapes don't mush to nothing, as one might expect. Instead they become plump and satin matte, like unpolished gem stones. The cooking liquor becomes a dark indigo; it too was revealed to squeals of surprise.

The trick with this dish is to reduce the cooking liquid before serving. That process intensifies the flavour and thickens the sauce, so it becomes more of a hearty stew than a dainty broth.

Preheat the oven to 200°C/180°C fan/gas mark 6.

Peel and roughly chop the onion and remove the grapes from their stalks.

Sprinkle a generous pinch of salt and pepper over the lamb and rub it in all over the surface of each shank. Heat 3 tablespoons olive oil in a heavy-based casserole over a high heat and, once the oil is hot, add the shanks. Fry on each side for a minute or so, until the skin is golden brown. Add the grapes, onion, rosemary and water to the pan. Bring the liquid to the boil and then cover everything with a disc of baking paper before clamping on a lid – if you don't have a lid, seal well with foil. Put into the oven and cook for 2 hours.

After this time, remove the shanks and some (about half) of the grapes and onions from the liquid and put onto a plate, covering with foil. Bring the liquid to the boil on the stove and reduce by about a half – you want it to be reasonably thick. Drain the beans, add those to the pan and cook to warm them through. Check the seasoning, adding a little more salt and pepper if required, and serve the lamb shanks on top of that purple, bean-studded stew.

SERVES
4

1 large onion

400g black grapes

4 lamb shanks

4 sprigs of rosemary

400g can black beans

Sea salt flakes
Coarse black pepper
Olive oil
400ml water

Five-hour Lamb with Potato Gratin

SERVES
6–8

A slow-roasted leg of lamb will always earn you a few gasps of surprise from whoever witnesses its unveiling. The flavour here not only comes from that slow-cooking process but also from the gutsy marinade of anchovies, garlic and mint; every single flake of lamb is gorgeous. The potatoes, sitting snuggly under the lamb, catch all of the meat's juices as it roasts and so become incredibly tender.

100g jar anchovies
in olive oil

8 garlic cloves

1 tablespoon
mint sauce

2kg leg of lamb

6 medium Maris
Piper potatoes

Sea salt flakes
Coarse black pepper

For the marinade, blitz the anchovies, and the oil they came in, with the peeled garlic cloves and the mint sauce to a smooth paste in a food processor. If you don't have a food processor you could make the paste using a sharp knife and bold ambition. Stir in 1 teaspoon each of salt and pepper.

With a sharp knife, stab the lamb leg repeatedly all over – you need as many deep cuts as possible, without completely massacring the meat. Spread the paste over the entire surface of the meat, working it well into the cuts. Refrigerate for an hour, or until required.

Preheat the oven to 160°C/140°C fan/gas mark 3. Remove the lamb from the fridge 1 hour before it goes into the oven, to bring it up to room temperature.

Slice the unpeeled potatoes as finely as possible – I use a mandoline – and arrange them in layers in a deep-sided roasting dish, seasoning with a very small pinch of salt and pepper every couple of layers. Place the lamb on top of the potato slices. Cover with a couple of sheets of foil, ensuring you seal it extremely well. Roast in the oven for 4½ hours.

Remove the dish from the oven and increase the heat to 220°C/200°C fan/gas mark 7. Remove the foil and baste the lamb with some of the juices from the roasting dish. Put everything back into the oven for a further 30 minutes. Remove the lamb from the oven, transfer it to a plate, cover it with foil and leave to rest. Return the potatoes to the oven for a final 25–30 minutes, until slightly crispy around the edges.

Lamb, Cherry and Yellow Split Pea Tagine

SERVES
4

As with most slow-cooked stews, the meat is so gently braised that, when cooked, it just flakes into tender pieces. The flavour combination here is somewhat of a cross-cultural mix: the ras el hanout is a North African spice blend (an exotic mixture of cardamom, cumin, cinnamon, rose and much more), while the cherry and lamb pairing is more Middle Eastern in its inspiration.

1kg diced lamb leg

2 tablespoons ras el hanout spice blend, plus extra for sprinkling

250g yellow split peas

175g dried sour cherries

1 unwaxed lemon

Olive oil
Sea salt flakes
Coarse black pepper
1 litre water

Preheat the oven to 160°C/140°C fan/gas mark 3.

In a large heavy-based saucepan or casserole – one you have a lid for – heat 1 tablespoon olive oil over a high heat. Once the oil is hot, add the pieces of lamb – it's probably best to do this in two batches – and fry until browned all over. Add the ras el hanout with a generous pinch of salt and pepper and stir to coat the pieces of lamb. Add the peas and cherries, stirring to coat them in the spices, then add the water.

Peel the zest from the lemon with a potato peeler – try to avoid getting too much white pith on the strips – and add the peel to the pan. Bring the pan to the boil, then cover with a lid or foil, and cook in the oven for 3½–4 hours – the lamb should be exceedingly tender and the peas cooked through. Do check the tagine after 2 hours and add a splash of water if it looks dry.

Serve in bowls, with a squeeze of lemon juice and a sprinkling of ras el hanout.

Variation

If you can't find the yellow split peas, just use green. Failing that, split lentils would be lovely, too. If the cherries are difficult to come by, dried cranberries would be a slightly more sour option, or use dried blueberries.

Mulled Wine Brisket with Roasted Cauliflower

When I think of slow cooking my mouth waters at the image of a beef brisket submerged in liquid and gently braised. The mulled wine here is first used for flavour – those subtle spices permeate into the meat – but also because its slightly acidic nature helps to break down the collagen in the meat, so you end up with something incredibly tender and tasty.

SERVES 4-6

Preheat the oven to 120°C/100°C fan/gas mark ½.

Finely slice the onions and add to a large casserole – one you have a lid for. Add the butter and a pinch of salt and cook over a medium heat until the onions start to sizzle. Reduce the heat to low and cook slowly, stirring occasionally, for 30 minutes, or until the onions are very mushy and caramelised. Remove the onions from the pan and increase the heat to high. Add the beef and sear for about a minute on each side.

Pour the wine over the meat and return the onions to the pan along with 1 teaspoon pepper. Bring to the boil, cover with a lid and slow-cook in the oven for 6–8 hours. You want the meat to be extremely tender; if you pull at a corner, it should flake away with little resistance.

Meanwhile, chop the cauliflower into medium-sized florets and chop the stalk into similar-sized pieces. Arrange in a roasting tray, drizzle with 2 tablespoons olive oil and add a pinch of salt and pepper. Mince the garlic and add to the tray, then toss everything together.

Once the meat is cooked, remove it from the oven and leave to rest, covered, in the pan. Increase the oven temperature to 210°C/190°C fan/gas mark 6. Roast the cauliflower in the oven for 35–40 minutes, tossing it every 15 minutes, until slightly charred and tender.

Remove the meat from the cooking liquor and cover with foil. Boil the cooking liquor, uncovered, until reduced by half. Season to taste, then serve – I shred the meat, but you can just serve it in hearty slices, if you prefer.

---

3 red onions

1.5kg unrolled beef brisket

750ml bottle mulled wine

1 large head of cauliflower

2 garlic cloves

50g unsalted butter
Sea salt flakes
Coarse black pepper
Olive oil

Ox Cheek in Port with Parsnip Mash

SERVES
4-6

Ox cheek is one of my favourite slow-cook cuts of beef. Because the cut is rich in collagen it makes for such a succulent stew. Sadly, its availability has declined in recent years, but a good butcher will have some in and if they don't, they'll happily order it for you.

The slow cooking and the reduction of the cooking liquor make this into a very rich stew, but with the addition of the vinegar-soaked onions, it's perfectly balanced.

1.5kg ox cheek

2 medium red onions

5 teaspoons
sherry vinegar

480ml ruby port

1.2kg parsnips

Sea salt flakes
Olive oil
Coarse black pepper
140g unsalted butter

Preheat the oven to 160°C/140°C fan/gas mark 3.

Slice each ox cheek into about 6 pieces and toss them with a pinch of salt. Peel and halve the onions and save one half for later. Slice the remaining three halves as finely as possible, and put into a bowl to one side until required.

Heat 2 tablespoons oil over a high heat in a heavy-based saucepan or flameproof casserole – one you have a lid for. When the oil is hot, add the ox cheek and fry for a few minutes until deeply coloured – you'll need to do this in two or three batches otherwise the meat won't brown. Once the meat is seared, put it onto a plate and set aside.

Add another tablespoon of oil to the pan along with the larger quantity of onions. Turn the heat down to medium–low and add 1 teaspoon of the vinegar and a pinch of salt. Fry the onions slowly, stirring frequently, for about 20 minutes, or until soft but not mushy.

Return the ox cheek to the pan with 2 teaspoons pepper and 450ml of the port. Bring the port to the boil, then cover and slow-cook in the oven for 3½–4 hours, or until the meat is beautifully tender – it should flake apart, but it should not be dry. Do keep an eye on the pan and check it after 2 hours: if it looks too dry, add a glug of water, though if your pan is any good it won't let too much moisture escape. And it's worth giving it a stir halfway through.

Slice the remaining onion half as finely as possible, put it into a small bowl with the remaining vinegar and a pinch of salt and set aside.

For the parsnip mash, peel the parsnips and cut them into even-sized chunks, pop them into a pan and cover with water. Bring to the boil and cook for 10–15 minutes, or until a knife pierces the flesh easily but they remain intact. Drain the water and return the parsnips to the pan, off the heat, with the butter and a pinch of salt and pepper. When the butter starts to melt, mash the parsnips roughly.

When the meat is cooked, remove the ox cheek from the pan with a slotted spoon, put it into a bowl and cover with foil to rest. Bring the cooking liquor to the boil over a high heat until reduced by a quarter, then stir in the remaining 30ml of port. Check the seasoning, adding more salt and pepper if necessary.

Serve a mound of parsnip mash topped with the ox cheek, a generous drizzle of the intense port sauce and the vinegar-soaked onion slices.

Variation
Red wine or cider vinegar would be acceptable alternatives to sherry vinegar.

POSH PLATES

IMPRESSIVE DISHES

I've never seen the value in meddling with ingredients so severely that they no longer resemble food. I find it exhausting; I'd much rather eat something bland-looking and totally moreish than something that looks spectacular but has been prodded and poked until it tastes of absolutely nothing. I've already expressed a deep-rooted disdain for 'molecular gastronomy' in this book (mocking inverted commas necessary here), but it bears repeating: that is not my idea of food. As a science or art form, yes, it can be impressive, but frankly I'd much rather do a tour of the Tate Modern whilst chowing down on a hotdog bought from a nearby vendor.

For me, all food has the inherent ability to evoke admiration. There are times in everyone's life when they want to do something a little bit special with food; we all long to be appreciated or loved. Food is the ultimate conveyer of love and, lucky for us cooks, it is the perfect tool to ensure that love and admiration are reciprocated.

But as well as having a softer, caring side, I am all too well versed in the art of one-upmanship. Sometimes it's just necessary. I'm not proud of this, you understand, but there have been times when I've wanted to blow little Miss Marvellous and her smorgasbord of dreams out of the water. And I've done just that; whilst food is mainly about love, it can be the ultimate weapon, too. I didn't poison her poussin or anything; I just put on a superior spread.

With all of that emotional turmoil in mind, and whatever your motive, this chapter should come as welcome reassurance for when you want to impress. That's not to say that the recipes here are sophisticated to the extent that they are impossible to recreate; it's important that the path of love or revenge is as smooth as possible. The dishes simply use slightly different ingredients that you might not expect to include on a day-to-day basis. One or two of these recipes may take a little more time than an everyday plate, but there's no secret or wizardry here; it's all just cooking.

Asparagus and Leeks Braised in Riesling and Tarragon with Prosciutto

SERVES
2

This is one of those suppers that is reasonably balanced but brings the smugness of both ease and comfort. The sweet Riesling, once evaporated and thickened, coupled with the gentle anise flavour of the tarragon, transforms the vegetables entirely.

You may notice I don't add any salt here. I just find that the reduced wine has such a startling body to it – and the prosciutto is salty enough – that additional salt would be overkill. But, your palate, your preference.

250g asparagus spears

180g baby leeks

200ml Riesling wine

5 sprigs of tarragon

8 strips of prosciutto

60g unsalted butter
Coarse black pepper

Trim the woody ends off the asparagus spears – I hold the root end in one hand, halfway up the stalk with the other, then gently bend it until it snaps. Wherever it breaks tends to be just about right. Rinse both the asparagus and the leeks, and dry completely with a clean kitchen cloth.

In a large, shallow casserole – one you have a lid for – heat 30g butter over a medium-high heat. Once melted, add the asparagus and leeks and fry, turning once, for a few minutes until gently coloured. I'm not bothered that the butter might burn here; in fact, those nutty qualities will enhance the dish.

When the vegetables are coloured, pour in the wine and throw in the tarragon with a pinch of pepper. Pop on the lid, reduce the heat to fairly low and simmer for 10 minutes. Once the wine has reduced almost entirely, and the vegetables are soft but with a gentle resistance, the dish is ready. Add the remaining butter in cubes and allow it to melt over the vegetables. Serve the asparagus and leeks with pieces of prosciutto draped in and amongst.

Roasted Radicchio and Figs with Stilton and Balsamic Onions

Radicchio, the Italian cousin of chicory, is incredibly bitter. Bitter enough, in fact, to bring a grimace to even the hardest-faced folk. But fear not, for when you roast this ruby-red leaf the flavour mellows and becomes slightly peppery. Layer that with pungent cheese and sweetly sour vinegar and you have something very special indeed.

SERVES
4

Preheat the oven to 200°C/180°C fan/gas mark 6.

Remove the outer leaves from the radicchio and cut it, through the root, into eight wedges. Arrange these in a medium-sized roasting dish.

Peel the onion and cut it into four wedges, leaving the root intact on each piece. Slice one piece as finely as you can manage – the sharper the knife, the better. Put the slices into a bowl, pour over the balsamic vinegar and leave to macerate until required.

Slice each of the remaining three quarters of the onion into four slithers and, it bears repeating, leave the root on each slither so that the onion layers hold together in each chunk. Put these into the dish with the radicchio. Quarter the figs and add to the dish, then pour over 3 tablespoons oil and add a generous pinch of salt and pepper. Toss everything together and roast for 15–20 minutes until the onions are fairly soft, the radicchio is wilted and the figs are mushy.

Crumble over the Stilton and return to the oven for a few minutes until the cheese melts. To serve, scatter over the macerated onions.

1 radicchio

1 large red onion

2 tablespoons
balsamic vinegar

4 figs

100g Stilton

Olive oil
Sea salt flakes
Coarse black pepper

Variation
If radicchio isn't available, you could use red chicory.
In which case, I'd use two chicory roots, slicing each into four lengthways.

Braised Fennel with Halloumi and Grapefruit

SERVES
2

Halloumi is one of those cheeses that satisfies – it is almost meaty. It's great as a lone snack, but here, with the gentle anise tones of fennel and the sharp tang from the grapefruit, it makes a refreshing plateful of food. What I love the most about this dish is how summery and fresh it all looks, though it could, of course, be served at any time of the year.

1 large fennel bulb

2 pink grapefruit

350g halloumi

2 tablespoons pine nuts

Small handful of mint leaves

Olive oil
Sea salt flakes
Coarse black pepper
30ml boiling water

Preheat the oven to 200°C/180°C fan/gas mark 6.

Remove the stalky fingers and leaves from the fennel – though do save the wispy fronds to use as a garnish. Chop the fennel bulb into about 16 wedges, leaving the root of each intact, pop them into a roasting tray and toss in 2 tablespoons olive oil and a pinch of salt and pepper. Add the boiling water to the tray, cover with foil and cook in the oven for 45–55 minutes, or until the fennel has really softened – have a nibble on a piece: if it's not quite soft enough to eat, cook it for a little longer. Once it is cooked, drain the fennel and allow to cool completely.

When the fennel is cool, peel and segment the grapefruit and toss together with the pieces of fennel.

Slice the halloumi into roughly 5mm-thick slices. Heat a frying pan over a high heat. Once the pan is hot, reduce the heat to medium and fry the halloumi slices for a minute on each side, or until charred and soft. Remove the halloumi from the pan, and use the same pan to quickly toast the pine nuts – just fry them over a high heat, tossing them occasionally, until lightly browned.

Lay the warm halloumi slices atop the fennel and grapefruit, scatter over the mint leaves, pine nuts and reserved fennel fronds, and finish with a good drizzle of olive oil.

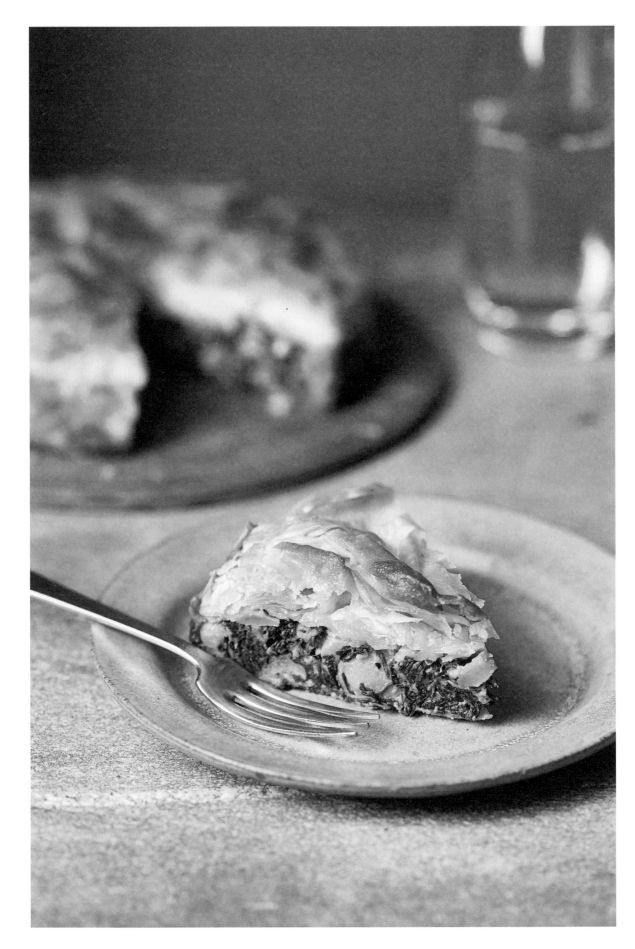

Squash, Gorgonzola and Rocket Spanakopita

Spanakopita, the classic Greek pie made with feta and spinach, is undoubtedly hard to compete with. My version here is totally off-piste in terms of flavour, but it is made, somewhat reassuringly, in the same way. And – dare I say it – I think this updated version gives the original a run for its money.

SERVES
4-6

Preheat the oven to 200°C/180°C fan/gas mark 6. Lightly grease a 20cm sandwich tin.

Peel the butternut squash and chop into 2cm chunks, discarding the seeds and pulp. Put the chunks into a baking tray and add 2 tablespoons olive oil and a generous pinch of salt and pepper and toss to coat well. Roast for 45 minutes until softened, then tip into a heatproof mixing bowl to cool.

Meanwhile, heat 1 teaspoon olive oil over a high heat in a large saucepan. Add the rocket – you may need to do this in batches – and stir-fry until completely wilted. Allow to cool until cold enough to handle, then put into a clean tea towel and squeeze out every last drop of moisture. Add to the roasted squash pieces and mix together. Pull the cheese into small chunks and add to the bowl along with the eggs and a pinch of salt and pepper. Mix until everything is well incorporated.

In a saucepan, heat the butter over a high heat until melted – don't let it brown. Unroll the sheets of filo pastry. Paint one sheet with a little melted butter and lay that, buttered-side-up, into the cake tin, allowing the surplus to overlap the sides of the tin. Repeat with the remaining sheets, laying each at a different angle to the next so that the entire tin is covered. Pile the filling into the tin, squashing it down lightly. Fold the surplus pastry up and over it to conceal it entirely, then paint with the remaining butter. Bake for 30 minutes, until the top is lightly golden and crispy.

This is great served warm or cold, but I would recommend you let it cool for 15 minutes or so. That way, the eggs set and the flavours mingle. You can cut it into small diamond shapes to serve, but I prefer a hearty triangular wedge.

750g butternut squash (about 1 small squash)

550g baby leaf rocket

180g Gorgonzola

2 large eggs

3 filo pastry sheets

Olive oil
Sea salt flakes
Coarse black pepper
75g unsalted butter

Gochujang Roasted Squash

SERVES
2-4

There is a wholesome balance to Asian flavours. Really, it's known as umami – that mouth-filling savouriness. Gochujang, which is a paste made from fermented chillies and soy beans, certainly delivers on the umami front. It's also rather spicy, which, when coupled with the sweet squash, is beautiful.

1 large
butternut squash

3 heaped tablespoons
gochujang

2 tablespoons
light soy sauce

3 spring onions

Small handful of mint

Olive oil
Coarse black pepper

Preheat the oven to 200°C/180°C fan/gas mark 6.

Peel the squash and cut it in half lengthways. Remove and discard the seeds, then slice the squash along the length into pieces about 1cm in thickness. Put the squash slices into a mixing bowl and add 1 tablespoon olive oil, a generous pinch of black pepper, the gochujang and soy and toss until well coated. Tip out onto a baking tray and bake for 45–50 minutes, or until the squash pieces are softened and ever so lightly charred – you can take them even further if you're partial to something a little more crispy.

Finely chop the spring onions and mint, scatter over the squash, then serve.

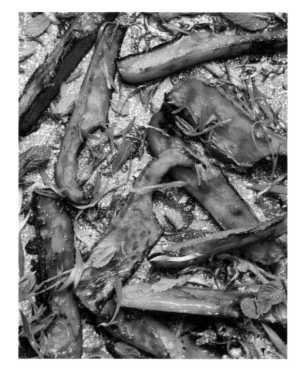

Variation
If you can't get your hands on squash, just use about 3 large sweet potatoes instead, cutting them into long, thin wedges.

Leftover ingredient
The gochujang goes so well in a sweet, shop-bought barbecue sauce. Just mix the two together at a ratio of 1:1 and use as a spicy dip for chicken and barbecued meats.

Brazil Nut and Gruyère Pesto with Shattered Lasagne Sheets

SERVES
4

With such reliably fabulous jarred varieties available, so many people rarely make their own pesto, but this version just isn't something you can find in the shops. The Brazil nuts give such a different flavour – obviously more nutty – and seem, in a way, to make the idea of pesto and pasta a much more wholesome affair.

For the pesto, grate the Gruyère and simply blitz it with the nuts, basil and peeled garlic in a food processor until blended. Then, with the processor still running, slowly pour in the olive oil. You should end up with a fairly smooth pesto.

Bring a large pan of water to the boil and add a large pinch of salt and 3 tablespoons olive oil. Smash the lasagne sheets into uneven shards and add to the water. Boil for 9 minutes, then drain – though do reserve 50ml of the starchy pasta water.

Return the cooked pasta to the pan and add the pesto. Heat over a medium heat for just a minute, until everything is warmed through. If at this stage the sauce looks a little scant or too thick, splash in some of the reserved water to loosen – though not too much. Serve the pasta with an extra drizzling of olive oil and a few chopped Brazil nuts.

45g Gruyère

60g Brazil nuts, plus extra to garnish

80g basil leaves

2 garlic cloves

400g lasagne sheets

150ml olive oil, plus extra for drizzling
Sea salt flakes
Coarse black pepper

Crab, Apple, Radish and Wasabi Pea Salad

SERVES
6

White crab meat just longs to be matched with fresh, slightly sharp ingredients. This salad is so refreshing but filling, especially if served to fewer people as heartier portions. I adore how the crab meat flakes into tiny white fronds and floats on top of the perfectly round, razor-thin slices of apple and radish.

This salad might sit ok in the fridge for a few hours, but the apples will inevitably start to oxidise and turn brown, so it's best to make this just before you want to serve it.

2 Royal Gala apples

8 radishes

Juice of 2 small limes

400g cooked white crab meat

50g wasabi peas

Sea salt flakes

Using a mandoline – or a sharp knife and a straight eye – cut the apples and radishes into very thin slices. Arrange the slices randomly on a large platter, squeeze over half of the lime juice and sprinkle with a pinch of salt.

Scatter the crab meat over the top of the apple and radish slices, then squeeze over the remaining lime juice – if the limes are particularly yielding, perhaps don't use all of the juice; you want this to be balanced and not too acidic.

Blitz the peas to a rough rubble in a food processor or put them into a ziplock bag and bash them with something hard. Sprinkle the peas over the salad and serve.

Miso and Lime Scallops with Soba Noodles

Speed and, of course, flavour are the main virtues of this dish. It's as wonderful tasting as it is simple and speedy to make. The miso delivers a certain punchy savouriness that is so well balanced with the sweet and sour honey and lime. Soba noodles are optional – any noodle would do – but I particularly like the nuttiness that the buckwheat flour gives.

SERVES
2

For the soba noodles, it's probably best to follow the packet instructions to cook them, which is probably along the lines of: plunge into a pan of boiling water and cook for 5 minutes. Drain the noodles and set aside until needed.

To make the sauce, simply stir together the miso paste, lime juice and honey in a bowl. Have this handy at the hob.

Heat 1 tablespoon oil in a frying pan over a medium heat. Once the oil is hot, add the scallops to the pan. Cook them for a minute on each side, then throw in the sauce and stir to coat. When cooking scallops don't try to yank them off the bottom of the pan; when they're ready to be flipped, they will allow you to turn them.

Pile the noodles onto a large plate and top with the cooked scallops and sauce, adding a pinch of salt and pepper.

200g soba noodles

100g miso paste

4 teaspoons lime juice

1 teaspoon
runny honey

6 king scallops

Olive oil
Sea salt flakes
Coarse black pepper

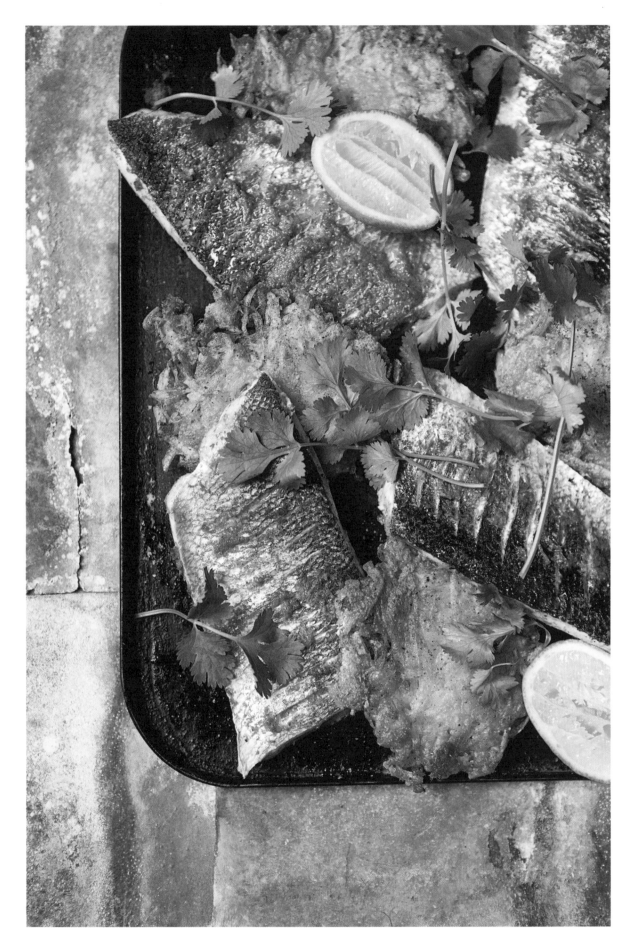

Red Curry Sea Bass with Potato Rosti

It's somehow reassuring that the coupling of fish and potato can take many different forms – each totally different – yet remain somehow familiar. This dish, unlike the deep-fried Friday-night version, is incredibly light, and that's thanks to (apart from the lack of batter) those bold spices in the red curry paste, along with the fresh lime and coriander.

SERVES
4

Preheat the oven to 200°C/180°C fan/gas mark 6.

Peel the potatoes before coarsely grating them into a clean tea towel or muslin cloth. Add a generous pinch of salt and pepper to the potatoes, tossing it through, then squeeze the towel as tightly as possible to remove all of the excess moisture from the spuds. Divide the potatoes into four portions.

Heat 3 tablespoons oil and the butter in a large frying pan over a high heat. Once the fat is hot, reduce the heat to medium. Form the potatoes into four very tightly compacted patties – pressing the rosti down into a chef's ring with a spoon would make far more sense, but I appreciate that equipment may be limited. Fry the rosti for 2–3 minutes on each side, then drain on a piece of kitchen paper and allow to cool for a few minutes.

Score the skin side of the fillets with four or five slashes and put them into a mixing bowl. Coat the fish fillets in the red curry paste along with a splash of oil and a pinch of pepper. Once they are well coated, place the fish onto a baking tray, along with the potato rosti, though don't overcrowd the tray; if you have to use 2 baking trays, do so. Roast for 12–15 minutes, until the fish is cooked through.

Serve the fish atop the rosti, scattered with some chopped coriander and a good squeeze of lime juice.

Leftover ingredient

Use leftover red curry paste for the Sweet Potato and Lentil Red Curry Soup on page 39.

2 large floury potatoes

4 sea bass fillets

3 tablespoons
red curry paste

Small handful of
fresh coriander

1 lime, cut into
wedges, to serve

Sea salt flakes
Coarse black pepper
Olive oil
50g butter

Cod with Pineapple Salsa

In Los Angeles, California, I had the best fish tacos served with a mango salsa. The combination of meaty white fish and the spicy, sweet and sour salsa was bizarre but beautiful. This recipe is inspired entirely by that meal, but I find the pineapple to be an improvement: it isn't as sloppy as the mango and so delivers that necessary sweetness with a good crunch. I have to follow the dish immediately with a tequila shot – any excuse.

½ medium pineapple

2 fat red chillies

Juice of 2 large limes

Small handful of fresh coriander

4 cod fillets

Sea salt flakes
Coarse black pepper
Olive oil

For the salsa, peel and core the pineapple and chop into small chunks, finely dice the chillies – I don't bother to deseed - and add both to a bowl with the lime juice. Finely chop the coriander and add to the salsa with a pinch of salt and pepper. Toss together and leave to macerate while you cook the cod.

Heat a frying pan over a medium–high heat and add 1 tablespoon oil. Sprinkle a little salt and pepper over the cod fillets and place them, skin-side-down, into the pan. Fry the fillets for 3 minutes, then flip them over and fry for a further 3 minutes. Remove the fish from the pan and allow to rest for a minute or two before serving underneath a generous amount of salsa.

Mackerel and Beetroot Salad

SERVES
4-6

This is a salad of opposites. The oily fish is a total contrast to the sweet beetroot, and the raspberry vinegar is just another disparate element. But put all those elements together and you have harmony. The sharp vinegar cuts through both the oiliness of the mackerel and the earthy sweetness of the beetroot. Dill is the ultimate counterpart to mackerel and beetroot and the hazelnuts offer something crunchy.

4 medium beetroot
(a variety of colours
works well)

300g cooked or
smoked mackerel fillets

3 tablespoons
raspberry vinegar

Small handful of dill

50g blanched
hazelnuts

Sea salt flakes
Coarse black pepper

Preheat the oven to 200°C/180°C fan/gas mark 6.

Wrap the beetroots individually, skins on, in foil and roast for 45 minutes. Remove from the oven and allow to cool completely. Once they have cooled, peel the beetroots and slice as thinly as possible – using a mandoline would make this much easier.

Arrange the beetroot slices onto a large platter and sprinkle over a pinch of salt and pepper. Flake the mackerel into mouthful-sized pieces and arrange over the beetroot. Drizzle over the vinegar and roughly chop the dill before sprinkling it on top of the salad.

Heat a dry frying pan over a high heat and, once it is hot, add the hazelnuts. Fry them, shaking the pan every few seconds, for just a minute or so – when you can smell the aroma of the toasting hazelnuts, they will be ready. Chop them roughly and scatter them over the salad.

Variations

For an express version of this salad, you could use ready-cooked beetroot. If you can't get hold of raspberry vinegar, balsamic would be a suitable alternative.

Ginger and Lime Spatchcock Poussin

SERVES
2

While a roast chicken is hard to compete with, these miniature versions are strong contenders: each person gets a full bird each, so it feels particularly fulfilling and grand. The trick to getting a lusciously golden, crispy-skinned poussin is to fry it before smothering it in sauce and roasting it. You could serve this with rice, but for me, one of these on its own is just about enough. I like to tear the flesh from the bones and dunk it into the sauce – using my fingers, of course.

2 poussins

35g piece of fresh root ginger

150g runny honey

50ml light soy sauce

1 lime

Coarse black pepper
Olive oil

To prepare the poussins, untruss them and remove the backbones with a sharp pair of kitchen scissors or a knife – cut to one side of the spine, from the parson's nose up to where the head would have been, and then repeat on the other side. Discard the backbone, lay the poussins, skin-side up, on a work surface and press heavily on the breast bone to flatten out the birds. Set aside until needed.

Preheat the oven to 200°C/180°C fan/gas mark 6.

For the sauce, peel and finely grate the ginger, then add it to a saucepan with the honey, soy sauce, zest and juice of the lime and a pinch of pepper. Bring to the boil, stirring to mix well, then remove from the heat and set aside until needed.

Place a large, ovenproof frying pan or shallow casserole over a high heat and add 1 tablespoon oil. Once the oil is hot, add the poussins, skin-side down and reduce the heat to medium. Cover with a piece of baking paper and weigh down with something heavy – another pan works well; the idea is to keep the birds as flat as possible. Fry for 5 minutes, then flip them over (discard the baking paper). Pour over the sauce and roast in the oven, uncovered, for 10-15 minutes, or until cooked through and the top is burnished and bubbling.

Variation
If you can't get hold of poussins, just use 4 skin-on, bone-in chicken thighs, frying those for only 3 minutes before smothering in the sauce and roasting.

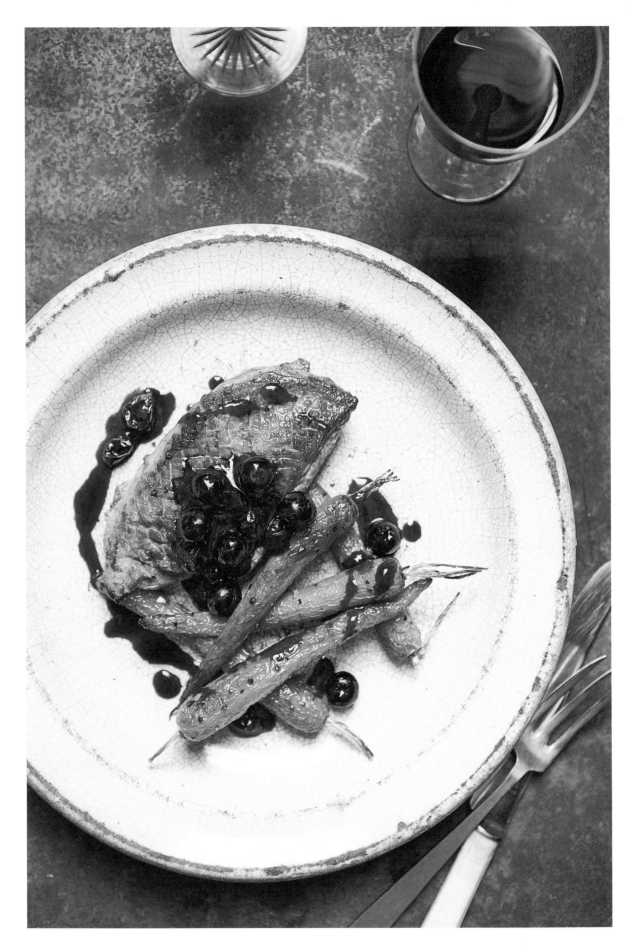

Duck Breast with Carrots and a Blueberry Hoisin Sauce

One thing that really surprises me is just how very few people have ever fried a duck breast. And when I ask them why, it's not because they don't like duck, but because they don't know how to cook it. The truth is, if you can fry a steak, you can fry a duck breast – it's just as easy. The trick is to just render down the fat first, which will give you a golden, crispy skin, but that takes no effort whatsoever.

SERVES
2

Preheat the oven to 220°C/200°C fan/gas mark 7.

Put the carrots, well spaced, onto a baking sheet or tray. Add 1 tablespoon oil and a pinch of salt and pepper, then toss together with your hands so they are all well coated. Roast for 25–30 minutes, until wrinkled and only very slightly charred.

Score the skin and fat of the duck breasts in a criss-cross pattern, then rub a little salt and pepper into the cuts. Heat a dry frying pan over a medium–low heat and, once it is hot, add the duck breasts skin-side down. Allow the gentle heat to render the fat down very slowly for 15–20 minutes. As the molten fat seeps into the pan, keep pouring it out into a mug or bowl. Once the skin of the duck is deeply golden and crispy, remove it from the pan.

Increase the heat of the pan to high and, as soon as it is hot, add a splash of duck fat and the butter. Place the breasts, skin-side up, into the pan. Cook them quickly, basting the tops with the hot fat and butter – tilt the pan slightly and scoop up the fat with a spoon, pouring it over the meat. Fry for just 2 minutes, then place the breasts onto a plate but don't cover them with foil – that will just ruin the crispy skin.

Pour the fat out of the pan, then add half of the blueberries along with the hoisin sauce and half of the lime juice. Cook over a medium heat until the blueberries break down to a thick, purple liquid, then add the remaining blueberries and stir to coat them in the juice. Remove from the heat and taste the sauce – if it needs more salt, pepper and/or lime juice, add accordingly.

Lay the duck breasts on top of the roasted carrots, spoon over the sauce and serve immediately.

250g long baby carrots (I like the ones that still have a little sprig of their tops)

2 duck breasts

100g blueberries

1 tablespoon hoisin sauce

Juice of 1 lime

Olive oil
Sea salt flakes
Coarse black pepper
50g unsalted butter

Ham and Fennel Pasta

Most would ordinarily assume fennel is best paired with fish, but that's not always the case; it's extremely versatile. Roughly chopped and thrown underneath a chicken before roasting, it softens and gently imparts flavour into the meat. Slowly fried, like onion, it sweetens and it retains its gentle anise flavour, which is delicious in this creamy pasta sauce with meaty nuggets of ham.

SERVES
2

Slice the fennel as finely as possible – I do this on a mandoline, but it can be done with a sharp knife if you protect your fingers. Save the wispy fronds to garnish. Add the sliced fennel to a large saucepan along with the butter, and set over a medium heat. Add a generous pinch of salt and pepper and stir until everything starts to sizzle. Reduce the heat to low and cook, stirring occasionally, until the fennel becomes extremely soft – a good 25 minutes.

Tear the ham into bits, add it to the pan and stir to coat. Pour in the cream and grate in the Parmesan. Stir until the cheese melts and you have a smooth sauce, then remove from the heat.

Bring a pan of water with a generous pinch of salt to the boil and add the pasta. Cook the pasta for 9 minutes until tender with just a little bite, then scoop out 75ml of the cooking water before draining the pasta. Return the drained pasta to the pan with the sauce and heat until warmed through, stirring in the reserved water if it looks a little dry. Serve immediately, and don't forget to scatter over those fennel fronds.

2 medium fennel bulbs

175g cooked ham

200ml single cream

50g Parmesan

200g large pasta
(I use lumaconi)

75g unsalted butter
Sea salt flakes
Coarse black pepper

Lamb Cutlets with Potatoes, Figs and Sherry

SERVES
4

It's so true that the meat closest to the bone is the most succulent. That's precisely what I adore about lamb cutlets: they are small nuggets of tender meat that just long to be nibbled on. Of course, if you prefer, you could make this with the slightly larger lamb chop, but you'd need to fry it for a minute or so longer on each side.

The fig and sherry combination is inspired by a tapas snack I ate in northern Spain years ago on a college trip. They called it 'higos rellenos' (stuffed figs), and although it was a sweet dish, that delicious marriage of figs and sherry is precisely what I loved with the lamb.

---

20 new potatoes

---

3 sprigs of rosemary

---

10 figs

---

8 lamb cutlets

60ml Amontillado
sherry

Olive oil
Sea salt flakes
Coarse black pepper

Preheat the oven to 200°C/180°C fan/gas mark 6.

Quarter the potatoes and scatter them over a roasting tray along with a good glug of olive oil and a teaspoon each of salt and pepper. Add the rosemary sprigs and toss everything together. Roast for 30 minutes, then halve the figs, add them to the tray and roast for a further 15 minutes.

Meanwhile, fry the lamb: rub about 1 tablespoon olive oil and a good pinch of salt and pepper into the cutlets. Heat a frying pan over a high heat and, once it is hot, add the cutlets, turning the heat down to medium. Fry for 4–5 minutes on each side. When the cutlets are cooked, transfer them to a plate and cover them with foil, then add the sherry to the pan (still on the heat) and stir to deglaze it and get all those meaty bits from the bottom of the pan. Allow the liquid to bubble up and reduce a little, add the juices from the rested meat then remove the pan from the heat.

Serve 2 cutlets per person with a hearty portion of the potatoes, 5 fig halves each and a good drizzle of the sauce.

Butterflied Lamb Leg with Aubergine, Yoghurt and Sultanas

A roasted hunk of lamb is an impressive thing, but it really couldn't be easier to cook – especially when the leg has been butterflied. This is something you can do yourself – just carefully run a sharp boning knife down and around the bone, freeing it from the meat – but, frankly, the butcher will do it in seconds for you.

Naturally the meat will be fairly uneven in width from one end to the other, so do bear that in mind when carving pieces, particularly for the fussy 'well-done fiends'.

SERVES
6–8

Preheat the oven to 220°C/200°C fan/gas mark 7.

Make a rub for the meat by mixing 1 tablespoon oil with 2 teaspoons each of salt and pepper and the hot smoked paprika. Rub this into the lamb leg, then place it, skin-side up, into a large roasting tray and leave to marinate while you prepare the aubergines.

In another roasting tray, simply rub the whole aubergines all over their skin with 1 tablespoon olive oil, and sprinkle with a little salt and pepper.

Roast the aubergines in the oven for 45 minutes and the lamb for 30. Though if you like your lamb particularly rare, you can pluck it out 5 minutes before that. The aubergines should be blackened somewhat and looking a little limp. Cover the lamb with foil and leave to rest until needed.

When the aubergines have cooled enough to handle, peel away the skins, then tear the flesh into long strips. Arrange these in a starburst pattern on a plate. Put the butter into a small saucepan and place over a high heat. Once the butter starts to foam like the head of a cappuccino and smells nutty, pour it over the aubergines. Drizzle over the yoghurt and scatter over the sultanas to serve. Slice the lamb thickly and plate up, drizzling over the meaty juices.

1.5kg butterflied lamb leg

---

2 tablespoons hot smoked paprika

---

4 aubergines

100ml natural yoghurt

75g sultanas

Olive oil
Sea salt flakes
Coarse black pepper
45g unsalted butter

MANY PLATES

DIPS, SALADS AND THINGS TO SHARE

One of my worst nightmares is turning up to a party where there isn't a scrap of food in sight – I've ostracised family members for far smaller misdemeanours. I'm not misguided or demanding – I don't expect more than a few dry, gristly canapés at a swanky drinks party; though if that is the case you can guarantee that I'll be the first to leave in famished pursuit of a burger bar or kebab house. And most likely harbouring a swiped bottle of bubbly, stashed in the arm of my overcoat, as compensation!

The way I see it is this: if life's major landmarks and milestones can be catered for, so can – and should be – any coming together, no matter how small. If families can provide buffets for a funeral wake when in the midst of mourning, there's no excuse for day-to-day life not to be catered for, too. It's all, in my eyes, part of a lifelong celebration. That may seem a crass argument, but food, ultimately, is life. In the main introduction to this book I noted that 'we've long since moved on from the primitive notion of food as fuel', and that's because food is not just for the body, but also for the soul. It's a sickly cliché, but I find it works. Food keeps us living, but good food keeps the party alive.

With that in mind, I wrote this chapter. The purpose here isn't to provide a load of recipes for those larger milestone occasions but to give you some ideas for food for everyday celebrations. That could simply be a solitary lunchtime at home – though perhaps just one or two of these dishes would suffice in that instance. A night in with friends and a bottle or two is the perfect excuse to put on a spread, as is an evening with all the family together at home at last.

But it's subjective: whatever your cause to celebrate, these recipes can be easily put together with little fuss. And as you dig into these plates, surrounded by those you love, your cheeks rosy from merriment (and perhaps pilfered booze!), somewhere inside your head a little voice will tell you: it's bloody good to be alive.

Cidery BBQ Ribs

A huge plate o'ribs will always signal the start of a feast. That refreshing informality of nibbling, with sauce-sodden fingertips, is what breaks the silence.

Often, ribs take hours of slow cooking, but here they're poached in cider, which speeds up the whole process. The added benefit of the cider is that this imparts a sour, apply tang to the meat; and if that's not enough, the acid tenderises the meat, too.

SERVES
4-6

Pour the cider into a fairly capacious saucepan and add a teaspoon of salt and the ribs. Bring to the boil, reduce to a simmer and cook the ribs for 25 minutes, skimming off the foam twice during cooking. Drain, reserving 150ml of cider.

For the sauce, put the ketchup, the reserved cider, the Worcestershire sauce, sugar and 1 teaspoon each of salt and pepper into a medium saucepan and stir to combine. Bring to the boil, then reduce to a simmer and cook for 10 minutes, or until thickened – you don't want it be very thick, just thick enough to coat the ribs and stay there.

When the sauce is ready, coat the ribs well with it – I use a heatproof pastry brush. Don't throw the leftover sauce away.

Preheat the oven to 240°C/220°C fan/gas mark 9.

Place the ribs on a baking sheet and roast for 15 minutes, basting with sauce halfway through. When the ribs come out of the oven, paint with the remaining sauce and serve.

1 litre dry cider

1.5kg pork ribs

250g tomato ketchup

60ml Worcestershire sauce

50g dark brown muscovado sugar

Sea salt flakes
Coarse black pepper

Mexican Party Corn

SERVES
8

Those Mexicans sure know how to party – and I'm not referring to the tequila here (though we all know a party fuelled with tequila is sure to get merry and messy!). Their food is awesome: the flavours are bold and brash and everything is prepared with love, but without fuss.

Elotes (corn on the cob) is a particularly popular Mexican street food. The boisterous mixture of cheese, lime and paprika marries so well with the sweet, toothsome corn. Ordinarily this is prepared on a barbecue, but I prefer the all-season oven method.

4 corn on the cob
(buy the ready-
peeled variety)

1 large lime

40g Parmesan

1 teaspoon
smoked paprika

Small handful of
fresh coriander

50g unsalted butter
Sea salt flakes
Coarse black pepper

Preheat the oven to 200°C/180°C fan/gas mark 6.

Slice the corn in half lengthways. This is more difficult than you might expect, because those cobs are tough little buggers; the best way is to stand the corn on its end and place a sharp knife on top. With one hand on the handle of the knife, and the other hand flattened and pressing down on the blunt edge of the blade, slowly seesaw the knife down through the cob. Don't try to rush this and please be careful; no corn is worth loosing a digit for. Place the corn, cut-side down, into a roasting dish just big enough to accommodate all eight halves snugly.

For the marinade, put the juice of the lime and butter into a small saucepan. Finely grate the cheese and add it to the pan, then heat everything over a high heat until it all melts together. The sauce will definitely look split, so please don't think you've done something wrong if it does. Pour this mixture over the top of the corn halves, then sprinkle over the paprika with ½ teaspoon each of salt and pepper.

Roast the corn, uncovered, in the oven for 30–40 minutes – the corn should be tender and the cheesy marinade slightly charred. Roughly chop the coriander and scatter it over just before serving.

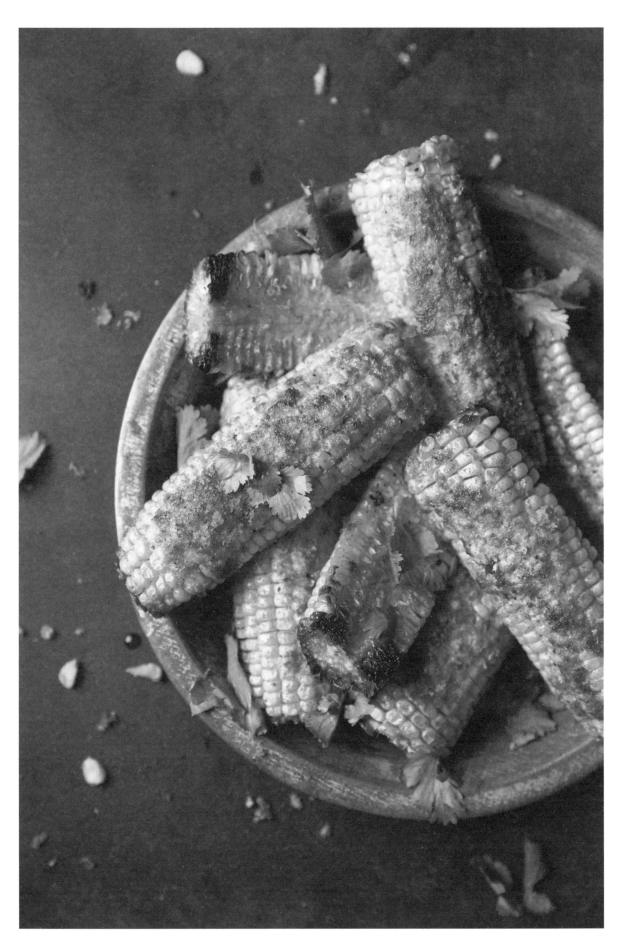

Spinach, Artichoke and Cheddar Dip

SERVES
8

This has to be my favourite dip. That's a bold statement, I know, and not one that I make without due consideration. There's something about the cheesiness of this paired with the unique flavour of the artichoke.

To make this even simpler than it already is, you could use frozen spinach (obviously defrost it before use), as that would cut out the entire wilting process – not that that's particularly time-consuming.

If there is any dip left over, it reheats beautifully with a quick blast in the microwave or in a saucepan over a medium heat.

250g spinach

1 large red onion

240g (drained weight) can or jar artichoke hearts

170g evaporated milk

170g Cheddar

Olive oil
Sea salt flakes
Coarse black pepper

First, wilt the spinach: pop it into a medium-sized saucepan with a splash of water and set it over a high heat. Stirring, cook the spinach down until it is wilted. Scoop it into a clean tea towel or muslin and allow to cool until cold enough to handle. Once it is cool, tightly squeeze the cloth to get rid of the excess water – you want the spinach to be really quite dry. Leave to one side until needed.

Chop the onion finely, add to the pan with 1 tablespoon oil and set over a medium heat. Stirring occasionally, cook the onion down for a good 10 minutes, until fairly soft but not coloured.

Put the onion, along with the spinach, drained artichoke hearts and 1 teaspoon each of salt and pepper, into a food processor and blitz very finely indeed – scrape down inside the food processor with a spatula if the mixture flies up the sides.

Return the mixture to the pan and add the evaporated milk. Grate the cheese and add that to the pan. Set over a medium heat and, stirring constantly, allow the cheese to melt. Decant into a serving bowl and dip to your heart's content. I serve this with tortilla chips, carrot slices and chunks of bread.

Blushing Hummus

SERVES
8–10

Hummus has become a famous staple dip across the world. It's easy to prepare and this version, made with shop-bought cooked beetroot, is somewhat sweeter than the original and much more colourful. Serve with tortilla chips or vegetable sticks, and your work is done in a matter of seconds.

This really couldn't be a more simple dip to prepare. Just throw 75ml oil, the beetroot, drained chickpeas (discard the liquid), the juice of the lime and Worcestershire sauce into a food processor fitted with a blade. Add a hefty pinch of salt and pepper and blitz to a smooth paste.

Serve in a bowl with a drizzling of olive oil, tear over the coriander and scatter with grated lime zest.

500g cooked beetroot

400g can chickpeas

1 lime

1 tablespoon Worcestershire sauce

Small handful of fresh coriander

Extra virgin olive oil
Sea salt flakes
Coarse black pepper

Big Bowl o' Spoon Salad

SERVES
6–8

The thing I love the most about this salad is how bejewelled it looks. Even though it's just a pile of everyday ingredients, there is something spectacularly beautiful about this dish, in both appearance and taste. The trick here is to ensure you dice everything as small, but as neatly, as possible; every spoonful should have a good selection of every ingredient on it.

75g currants

2 large aubergines

500g mixed-colour tomatoes

30g flat-leaf parsley

1 tablespoon sumac

Olive oil
Sea salt flakes

Put the currants into a heatproof bowl and pour over boiling water to cover. Leave to soak for 5 minutes or so.

Chop the aubergines into tiny dice, as small as you can humanly manage without turning them to mush. Heat 3 tablespoons of oil in a frying pan over a high heat and, once the pan and oil are hot, add the aubergine and stir-fry for just 1 minute until the pieces are slightly charred. Remove from the heat and tip into a salad or mixing bowl.

Dice the tomatoes as finely as possible – again, you don't want to pulp these; the aim is to achieve tiny little chunks. Add to the bowl with a generous pinch of salt, and toss together. Allow everything to macerate for 30 minutes or so.

Just before serving, roughly chop the parsley and add it to the bowl, along with the sumac. Drain the currants of the excess water and toss them through the salad. Drizzle over a little olive oil if you think it needs it – though the salt should have drawn plenty of juice from the tomatoes.

Focaccia and Infused Oil

A homemade focaccia will always impress. There's something rewarding about bread that you have made yourself, even though it's really exceedingly simple. It feels as though you've achieved something: a creation to be proud of. And, even better, when people devour the loaf with impressed gratitude it's a win-win situation.

SERVES
10-12

To make the focaccia dough, toss together the flour with 10g salt and the yeast. Add 400ml water (tap water is fine) with 50ml of the olive oil, bring together into a very sticky dough, then knead until the dough is very elastic and smooth. You can battle with this by hand, slapping the dough down onto and around the worktop, but it's so darn sticky that using a freestanding mixer fitted with a dough hook and set on a medium speed is far easier.

Once the dough is sufficiently kneaded, coat with a little oil and leave to rest in a warm place until the dough has ballooned up and tripled in volume – up to 1 hour.

While the dough rises, infuse the oil. Finely chop the tomatoes and put them into a bowl. Slice the garlic cloves finely and place them into a pan with the remaining 100ml oil and set over a low heat. Allow to infuse for just a minute, then cool slightly before pouring the oil over the tomatoes. Roughly chop the parsley leaves (chop the stalks finely) and add to the oil with 1 teaspoon each of salt and pepper.

When the dough has risen, oil a medium, deep-sided roasting tray well and gently tip the dough out into it, being careful not to deflate it too much. Lightly tug the dough into a very rough rectangle and allow to rise again until almost doubled in size – up to 1 hour.

Preheat the oven to 240°C/220°C fan/gas mark 9. Dip your first and middle fingers into flour and prod holes all over the surface of the focaccia, ensuring you press your fingers right down to the baking tray below. Bake for 25–30 minutes, until golden brown and crispy, then remove and leave to cool.

To serve, slice the focaccia into long, thin chunks and scatter the infused oil on top.

500g strong white
bread flour, plus
extra for dusting

14g fast-action
or instant yeast

12 cherry
vine tomatoes

3 garlic cloves

Handful of
flat-leaf parsley

Sea salt flakes
400ml water
150ml olive oil, plus
extra for greasing
Coarse black pepper

My Favourite Tomato Salad

SERVES
6–8

Call me old-fashioned – which this salad most certainly is – but sometimes it's the classics that are most fulfilling. With strongly aromatic tomatoes and sweetly pungent shallots, this is easily assembled and completely satisfying.

As a rule of thumb, when shopping for tomatoes I always give them a good sniff. They should have a strong, sweet scent. If they don't smell of anything, leave them on the shelf. You may look a little odd and receive a few enquiring glances, but when you get them on the table the result is worth it. Any onlookers will be forever doomed to their insipid tomatoes while you revel in your flavoursome selection.

2 banana shallots

4 tablespoons sherry vinegar

1 tablespoon caster sugar

500g mixed-colour heritage tomatoes

Small handful of flat-leaf parsley

Sea salt flakes

Slice the shallots as finely as you can manage into very thin discs, and pop them into a bowl with the vinegar and sugar. Leave to macerate for a good 30 minutes.

Slice the tomatoes thinly and arrange them randomly on a large platter. Sprinkle with a generous pinch of salt, then dress with the soaked shallots. Finely chop the parsley and scatter over the top.

Watermelon, Cucumber and Strawberry Salad with a Gin Splash

SERVES
6-8

Imagine yourself on a hot, humid day: the ice in your drink clatters as beads of condensation bejewel the glass, mimicking the pricks of sweat on your brow. Now imagine a salad so refreshing that it bursts with every bite. So refreshing that one single mouthful cools you instantly. Well, here it is.

Cut the watermelon into thin triangles – each about 4mm in thickness. Hull the strawberries and slice them thinly. Slice the cucumber thinly, too. Arrange the slices randomly on a large platter. Drizzle the gin over the slices. Finish with a small pinch of salt and pepper, toss together and serve, scattering over the mint leaves. If you leave this for an hour or so at room temperature it gets even better.

250g watermelon

175g strawberries

¼ cucumber

2 tablespoons gin

About 10 mint leaves, shredded

Sea salt flakes
Coarse black pepper

Variation
If you're serving this to children and can't bear the thought of slightly tipsy ratbags, substitute the gin for freshly squeezed lime or orange juice.

Tempura Cocktail Sausages with Hoisin Dip

SERVES
6-8

When I was growing up, my parents ran a fish and chip shop, and I was always intrigued when someone asked for a battered sausage – I never liked sausages or batter. But now my palate has matured, the concept truly is a delicacy for me.

This recipe is Anglo-Asian: the battered sausage is certainly British, whilst the tempura and hoisin dip remind me of the East.

130g tempura
batter mix

30 cocktail sausages
(uncooked)

150g hoisin sauce

1 tablespoon
fish sauce

Juice of 1 lime

180ml water
1.5 litres frying oil

To make the batter, tip the batter mix into a mixing bowl and make a well in the centre. Whisking constantly, slowly pour the water into the flour, to create a smooth batter. Leave it to rest for 5 minutes or so.

Heat your oil in a heavy-based saucepan or wok to 180°C – though if you've got a deep-fat fryer, just use that. If you've neither fryer nor thermometer, the oil will be ready when a cube of bread dropped into it sizzles and floats – though keep an eye on the heat so that you don't burn everything.

Have ready a large plate covered with a few layers of kitchen paper, to drain the sausages on after frying. Dredge the sausages through the batter, shaking off the excess, then drop them into the hot oil – you might need to do this in batches to avoid overcrowding. Fry for 5–7 minutes, until the batter is golden brown and crispy. Spoon them out – a slotted spoon is the best tool for this – and drain on the paper-lined plate.

For the sauce, simply mix the hoisin, fish sauce and lime juice together and you're ready to dunk and devour.

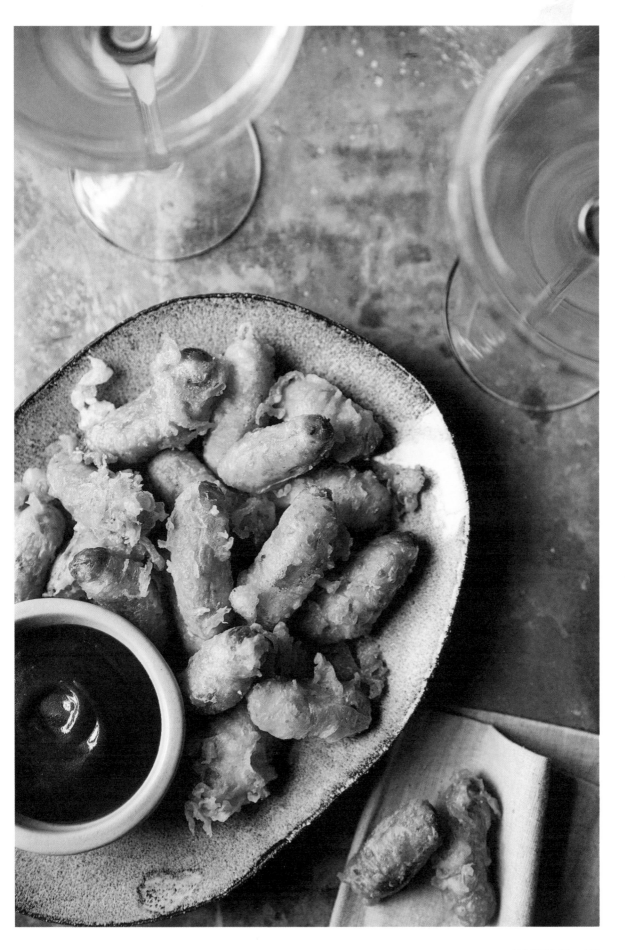

Middle Eastern Lamb Nachos

SERVES
6-8

Real party food is the sort of stuff you just have to keep going back to, emboldened by the booze and against the judgement of others. That's true in my case, anyway. But these really are sensationally good, and so different from the boring old chips 'n' dips you'd expect to stumble upon at a disco spread.

The idea is, based on the chapter title, that these are for sharing with a crowd, but this recipe would make a lovely midweek supper too.

---

6 pitta breads

500g lamb mince
(20% fat)

---

2 tablespoons sumac,
plus extra to finish

---

1 small pomegranate

100g feta

Sea salt flakes
Coarse black pepper
Olive oil

Preheat the oven to 220°C/200°C fan/gas mark 7.

Cut the pitta breads into bite-sized triangles – I cut each one into about 6 – and place them, well-spaced, onto a large baking sheet. Once the oven is hot, bake the pitta pieces for 15 minutes until crisped up and ever so slightly browned. Remove the sheet from the oven but leave the pitta pieces on it to crisp even more as they cool.

In a mixing bowl, mix together the lamb and sumac with 1 teaspoon each of salt and pepper and 3 tablespoons olive oil – I use my hands to squelch everything together so that it's all perfectly mixed.

Heat 1 tablespoon olive oil in a frying pan – one you have a lid for – over a high heat. Once the oil is hot, add the lamb mince and fry, turning once, until lightly browned. Cover with the lid to trap in the steam. Reduce the heat to low and cook for 15 minutes – the lamb should be flavourful and tender and there should be a little bit of juice in the pan.

Scatter the pitta pieces around the serving plate and scatter the spiced lamb over the top. Top with the seeds from the pomegranate (I slice the pomegranate in half, hold one half cut-side-down over the plate and bash the topside with the back of a wooden spoon, scattering seeds and juice on top of the lamb). Finish by crumbling over the feta and adding an extra sprinkling of sumac.

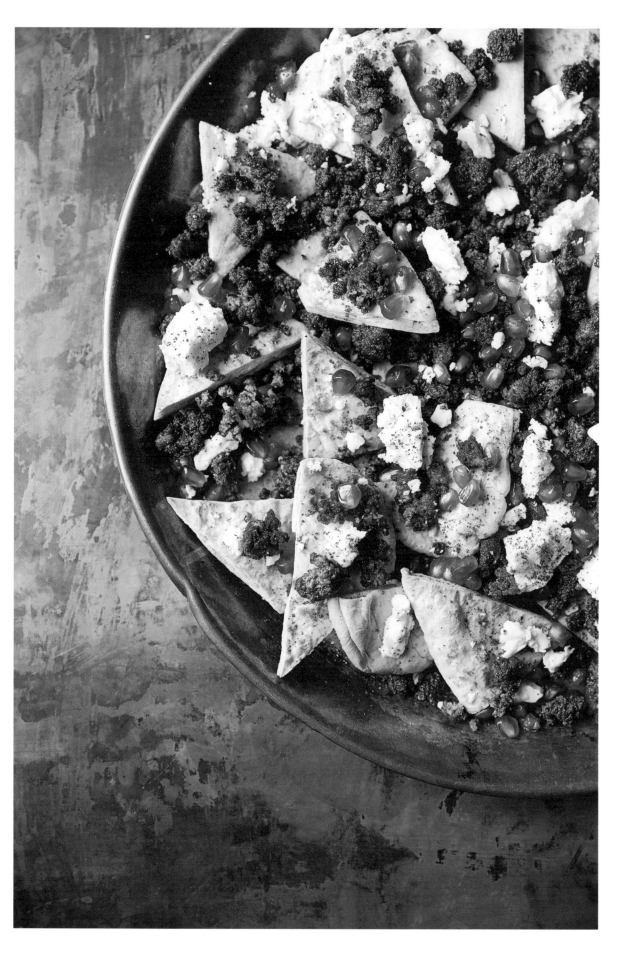

Beetroot and Anchovy Galette

SERVES 6–8

I'm a sucker for ready-prepared beetroot, the kind that dyes your hands bright pink and tastes earthy and sweet. Couple that flavour with the punchy saltiness of anchovies and that somewhat strange herbal quality of oregano, and you've got an instantly gratifying combination.

320g packet ready-rolled puff pastry (all-butter is best)

500g cooked beetroot (the kind in vacuum packs)

100g anchovies from a jar

2 teaspoons oregano, plus a little extra to garnish

30g Parmesan

Sea salt flakes
Coarse black pepper

Preheat the oven to 200°C/180°C fan/gas mark 6.

Unroll the pastry onto a baking sheet and score a 1cm margin all around the edge with a knife. Slice the beetroot as finely as possible and set the slices onto the pastry in neat lines, overlapping slightly, within the scored margin.

Drain the anchovies and lay them over the beetroot in criss-crossing lines, then roughly chop and scatter over the oregano and a pinch of salt and pepper. Bake the galette for 30–40 minutes, or until the pastry has puffed up. Finely grate the Parmesan and sprinkle it, plus a little extra oregano before serving.

Variation
If you're not keen on anchovies you could swap them for chopped, pitted black olives.

Pickled Cucumbers with Nigella Seeds and Goat's Cheese

SERVES
4

Cheese and pickle is, as most of us know, a match made in heaven. This is just a different way of offering that holy union. Served for lunch or just as a side salad at a feast, the flavour of the nigella seeds with the sweet-sour pickle is intriguing and delicious.

With a potato peeler or mandoline, slice the cucumbers into thin ribbons and arrange them randomly on a large plate.

In a small saucepan, heat the cider vinegar, sugar and nigella seeds, bringing it to the boil, then simmering gently for just 2 minutes to let the flavours infuse. Pour the pickling liquid over the cucumber slices, sprinkle with a pinch of salt and allow to rest at room temperature for a good hour.

Carefully crumble the cheese into small nuggets and scatter over the plate of pickled cucumbers before serving.

Variation
Fennel seeds, in place of the nigella, offer a strong anise flavour; though I'd only use 2 teaspoons of these rather than a tablespoon.

2 cucumbers

80ml cider vinegar

45g caster sugar

1 tablespoon
nigella seeds

120g soft
goat's cheese

Sea salt flakes

SWEET PLATES

CAKES, PUDDINGS AND DESSERTS

There's a magic to baking that isn't required in general cookery. While both involve the bringing together of ingredients to produce a final something, the two processes are actually incomparable. In cookery, for the most part, the individual ingredients don't stray far from their original form: a carrot becomes a roasted carrot; a duck breast becomes a pan-fried duck breast; a leg of lamb remains a leg of lamb. In that process, you are in complete control of how those ingredients will slightly alter. You can adjust the heat of the pan, and you can quickly whip something out of the oven if it's looking a little overdone. When making a stew or soup, you taste and season as you go, and bland dishes can always be rescued with additional splashes of this and that.

But baking isn't quite so reliant on intuition or a trust in one's own palate: it is a form of alchemy. It's enchanting how a few ingredients can form a beige batter, which in turn will metamorphose into a golden brown, sugar-dusted masterpiece. As part of that sorcery, there is a great mysterious anticipation as to whether the flour, eggs, butter and sugar you mix together will come out of the oven resembling anything near to a cake. But that's all part of the excitement, because when you find yourself nibbling on a wedge of jam-filled Victoria sponge, you do so with a sense of smugness and pride – I created this. This mysterious quality isn't intended to evoke deep feelings of fear; the process is an exciting one involving an element of surprise. I suppose that's why cakes – even lopsided sponges with gaudy sprinkles – will always be met with gasps of surprise and marvel.

But aside from the pride and sorcery, it's impossible to deny that baking is a great bringer of comfort. The entire process, from weighing to devouring, takes me back to childhood and the cosy, warming protection of the kitchen and my family.

Caramelised Bourbon and Peanut Butter Crème Brûlée

MAKES
4

A crème brûlée is a relatively small portion of dessert – the pot confines the serving size, unlike a personally portioned wedge of cake – so it should make a long-lasting impression. My version of this classic dish is decadent and delightful in equal measure, with the gentle warming quality of Bourbon and a sweet nuttiness from the peanut butter.

160g caster sugar

500ml full-fat milk

30ml Bourbon whiskey

5 large egg yolks

100g smooth
peanut butter

Preheat the oven to 160°C/140°C fan/gas mark 3. Have four 175ml (approx.) ramekins and a deep-sided roasting dish ready and bring a kettleful of water to the boil.

Heat a medium saucepan over a high heat and, once it is hot, reduce the heat to medium. Add 100g of the sugar to the pan and let it slowly melt and caramelise – you want a dark amber colour. You can stir the sugar as it starts to melt, but don't overdo it as it could crystallise. An easier, but longer, way to get a caramel is to add 100g sugar to a cold saucepan with 4 tablespoons cold water. Dissolve the sugar in the water, then set over a high heat and bring to the boil without stirring at all. Allow the water to boil away until the mixture thickens and becomes the dark amber required.

Once you have made a caramel, reduce the heat to low and add the milk a drop at a time, whisking well. The cold milk will cause the hot mixture to bubble and spatter, but stand back a little, ignore this and carry on carefully. If you add the milk too quickly, the caramel will solidify and you'll need to stir for a while for it to dissolve. Once the milk is incorporated and fairly smooth, add the Bourbon and bring to the boil, then remove from the heat.

Whisk the egg yolks in a mixing bowl until smooth and pale, then add the peanut butter a spoonful at a time, beating vigorously after each addition using a wooden spoon, as this will be incredibly thick, until smooth. (If you add the peanut butter all in one go, it will be very difficult to get a smooth mixture.)

Swap back to the whisk and add the hot milk mixture, a drop at a time, to the egg mixture while whisking constantly. This does require elbow grease and patience. Remember: it's easier to get any large lumps out while the mixture is still fairly thick; once you've added all the milk it's far more difficult to get a smooth texture. Once it is all incorporated, pass the custard through a fine sieve into a jug, then divide between the four ramekins.

Put the ramekins into the deep roasting dish and pour in boiling water so that the surface of the water is three-quarters of the way up the ramekins. Bake in the oven for 40–45 minutes, until the crème brûlée just trembles ever so slightly in the centre. Allow to cool, then cover and refrigerate for 2 hours; though overnight is best.

Before serving, preheat the grill and sprinkle the remaining 60g sugar over the top of each crème brûlée. Toast the puddings under the grill, just until the sugar melts and caramelises. If you have a chef's blowtorch, use that instead of the grill.

Variation
If you don't drink Bourbon but have a stockpile of cheap whisky, rum or brandy – gifts from thoughtless family members – just use any of those instead.

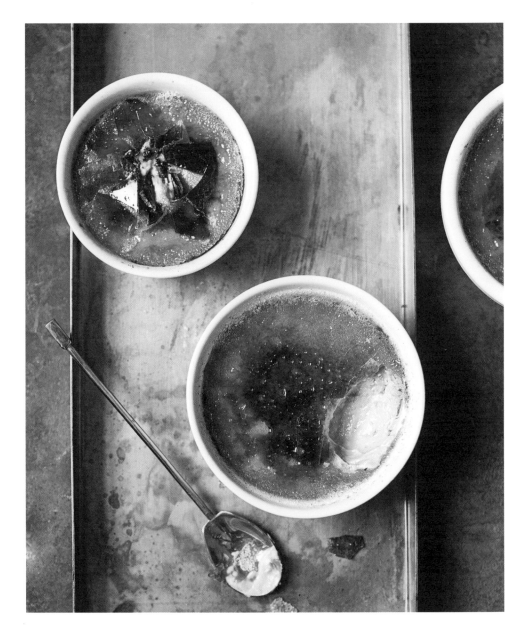

Rosewater and Nutmeg Pearl Barley Pudding

SERVES
6-8

I first had something along these lines in Stevie Parle's Greenwich restaurant, Craft. It's bizarre, weird and totally wonderful. It has the reassuring homeliness of a sweet rice pudding, but that's almost contradicted by the otherworldly scent and spice of rose and nutmeg.

200g pearl barley

125g light brown muscovado sugar, plus a little extra for topping

600ml single cream

2 tablespoons rosewater (I use the brand East End, and it is just right)

1 teaspoon freshly grated nutmeg

Put the pearl barley in a sieve and give it a good rinse under cold water until the water runs clear. Transfer the barley to a saucepan and cover with a good few centimetres of water. Bring to the boil, then reduce to a simmer and cook for 35–45 minutes, or until the barley is plump and completely soft. You'll probably need to keep an eye on the water level and top it up if the pan is threatening to dry out.

Meanwhile, mix the sugar with the cream, rosewater and nutmeg.

Preheat the oven to 200°C/180°C fan/gas mark 6.

When the pearl barley is ready, drain off any excess water and pulse it in a food processor into a finer grain. Add this to the cream mixture and stir well so that everything is evenly mixed. Pour into a 23cm pie dish or cake tin (not a loose-bottomed one, for obvious oozing reasons) and bake in the oven for 50–55 minutes until thick and set. Remove from the oven and sprinkle over a little extra sugar while the pudding is still hot.

Fennel-seed Poached Pear with Chocolate Sauce and Caramelised Oats

MAKES
4

Pears and chocolate are a combination that takes me right back to school dinners. Everything else about those sloppy meals – apart from potato croquettes and ketchup – has slipped from my memory, but pears and chocolate are etched merrily into my mind. This is a slightly more mature version, with the fennel seeds offering a gentle liquorice tone to it all.

30g rolled oats
450g caster sugar
3 tablespoons fennel seeds
4 Comice pears
150g dark chocolate (80% cocoa solids)
700ml water

For the caramelised oats, heat a frying pan over a high heat. Once the pan is hot, add the oats and toss them to toast for just a minute. Add 50g of the sugar and allow it to melt slowly and coat the oats. Once the caramel is a gentle golden amber, pour the oats onto a plate and allow to cool and harden.

Put the water, remaining sugar and the fennel seeds into a saucepan big enough to comfortably fit the 4 pears. Stir to almost entirely dissolve the sugar. Peel and core the pears, though leave them whole with their stalks intact. Add them to the pan and set the heat to high. Once the syrup starts to boil, reduce to a gentle simmer and cover the pears with a disc of baking paper – I just tear a square off, scrunch it up, unwrap it, then tuck it over the pears. Simmer the pears until a knife easily pierces the flesh but they remain whole and not sloppy – about 20 minutes. Remove the pan from the heat and allow the pears to cool in the poaching liquid for 5 minutes.

Meanwhile, roughly chop the chocolate and put it into a heatproof mixing bowl. Remove the pears from the pan using a slotted spoon and transfer to a plate. Measure out 120ml of the pear poaching syrup and bring that back to a simmer. Pour the simmering syrup over the chocolate, leave it for 10 seconds to melt the chocolate, then whisk to a smooth, glossy ganache.

Place each pear onto a plate and pour over a generous glug of the ganache.

Waste not, want not
Don't throw away the leftover syrup; it's so beautiful added, in moderation, to vinaigrettes for salads, or used as syrup for cocktails.

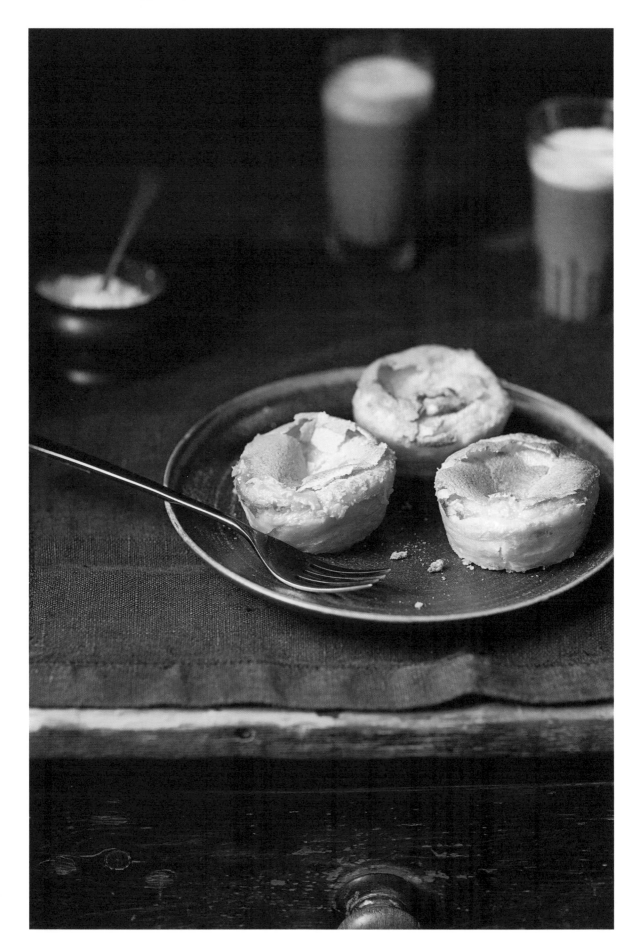

Apple Custard Tarts

The real origin of these flaky little morsels is entirely down to my own flakiness. During an afternoon of Portuguese-custard-tart baking I couldn't be bothered to trundle to the shops for more eggs, so I scoured the cupboards in hope. It was either apple sauce or wholegrain mustard as an alternative... Without the courage to be quite so daring, I used the apple sauce – and I'm truly glad I did.

MAKES
12

Preheat the oven to 220°C/200°C fan/gas mark 7 and grease a deep 12-hole muffin tray well.

Dust the worktop rather liberally with icing sugar, then unroll the pastry onto it and sprinkle it with more icing sugar. Roll the pastry back up tightly – you might need to wet the top edge with just a little water so it sticks and stays rolled. Slice into 12 even discs – I cut it in half, then cut each half in half, then cut those quarters into three chunky discs.

Stand a disc of pastry up on one of its flat cut sides, then squash it down with the heel of your hand. With a rolling pin, roll it out into a disc big enough to tuck messily into the muffin tray. Press it into the tin, lining the muffin hole, and then repeat with the remaining portions of pastry until each hole of the tray is lined. If you're working in a hot kitchen, it might be a good idea to keep the chunks of pastry in the fridge, then once all cavities in the tray are lined, pop the whole tray into the fridge for 10 minutes or so.

Divide the apple sauce between the pastry cases. For the custard filling, whisk together the icing sugar and egg yolks until the sugar dissolves, then whisk in the cream until combined. Pour the custard into the pastry cases – I find it easier to put the custard into a jug first, then carefully pour it over the apple sauce. Leave a millimetre or two of pastry clear at the top, as the custard will rise quite dramatically.

Bake in the oven for 20 minutes. The custard will darken on top and sprout up over the pastry – and please don't worry if the tarts look cracked, it's all part of their charm. Remove the tarts immediately from the tin and set on a wire wrack to cool. Finish with an extra dusting of icing sugar.

80g icing sugar, plus extra for dusting

320g ready-rolled all-butter puff pastry

250g Bramley apple sauce

5 large egg yolks

80ml single cream

Oil, for greasing

Eastern Fruit Salad

SERVES
2-4

This is so beautiful – both to behold and to devour – that it seems almost otherworldly. It isn't strictly a fruit salad as it contains sweets and nuts, but I couldn't care less what the purists say; I'm emboldened by the beauty of this salad. The flavours, as you can imagine, are both light and complex all at once. The mixture of sharp raspberries and sweet Turkish delight contrasts so well with the mellow figs and salted pistachios.

4 figs

2 tablespoons orange blossom honey

150g raspberries

100g salted roasted pistachios

200g lemon and rose Turkish delight

Preheat the oven to 220°C/200°C fan/gas mark 7.

Cut each fig into eight segments and arrange them in a small roasting dish. Drizzle the figs with the honey and roast them for just 10 minutes, until softened, then remove from the oven and allow to cool completely in the roasting dish.

Arrange the figs on a large serving plate. Chop some of the raspberries in half – use a very sharp knife so you don't squish them – and scatter these and the whole raspberries in and among the fig slices. Remove the pistachios from their shells and chop them roughly, then scatter those on the plate, too. Finally, cut the Turkish delight into small nuggets and add to the plate. Eat immediately.

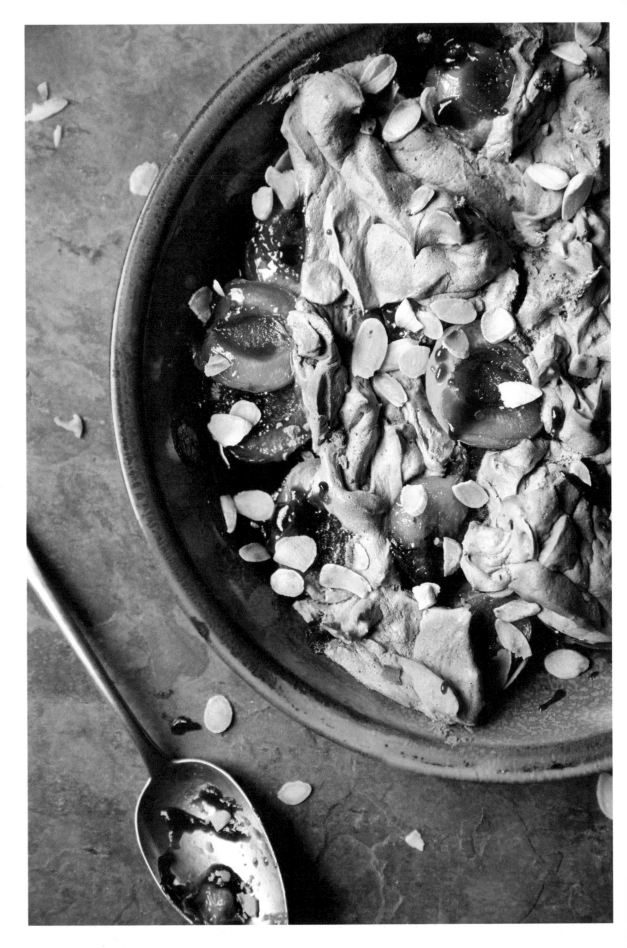

Amaretto Apricots with Brown-sugar Meringue

Deep, golden orange apricots are such a delicious fruit. Although their flavour is primarily of sweet nectar, it comes with a faint tartness which I adore. They are so perfectly paired with the almond tones of amaretto, and the mellow sweetness and yielding crunch of a brown sugar meringue.

SERVES
4

Preheat the oven to 220°C/200°C fan/gas mark 7.

Halve the apricots, remove their stones and place them cut-side up in a medium-sized roasting dish. Cut the butter into small dice and scatter it over the apricots. Sprinkle over the liqueur and 20g of the sugar and bake for 20–25 minutes, until the apricots soften and just start to colour very slightly.

While the apricots roast, make the meringue. Whisk the egg whites to stiff peaks, then add the remaining sugar a tablespoon at a time whilst whisking constantly until you have a very thick, glossy meringue. I do this on high speed in my freestanding electric mixer fitted with the whisk attachment, but it can be done just as easily with a handheld electric mixer. Fold the flaked almonds into the meringue, being careful not to deflate the mixture.

Once the apricots have roasted, randomly splodge the meringue over the top of them and sprinkle over more almonds, then return to the oven for a further 15–20 minutes, until the meringue is coloured and slightly crispy on top, and a golden satin matte.

12 fresh apricots

90ml amaretto liqueur

195g dark brown muscovado sugar

3 large egg whites

50g flaked almonds, plus extra for sprinkling

60g unsalted butter

Variation

You could experiment with other stone fruits, but always try to select the firmer options as watery fruits could turn into a soggy mess in the heat of the oven.

Blackberry and Bay Brown Butter Tart

SERVES
8–10

Brown butter tarts are heaven. Imagine the butterscotch sweetness of fudge with the dense, rich texture of a brownie and you're almost there. Encase all of that – if you haven't already passed out in ecstasy – in a golden sweet pastry and you have something impossibly indulgent. My version welcomes the sharp blackberries and the haunting, lingering flavours of bay. I use dried bay leaves here, but bear in mind that they do quickly lose their flavour when they sit unused in their jars.

The pastry method here is much more American than continental – French traditionalists, look away now. Not only is it a brown sugar pastry, and so is much darker than usual, it's also just squidged into the tart tin rather than carefully rolled out. It makes life a hell of a lot easier.

220g light brown muscovado sugar, plus a little extra for sprinkling

4 large eggs

300g plain flour

3 dried bay leaves

150g blackberries

280g unsalted butter, plus extra for greasing
Sea salt flakes

Very lightly grease a 23cm fluted tart tin.

I make the pastry in my freestanding electric mixer fitted with the paddle attachment, but you could do it with a handheld electric beater – or even a wooden spoon if you're feeling strong! Beat 100g of the butter with 50g of the sugar until very smooth and pale. Beat in 1 of the eggs, incorporating it well, then toss in a pinch of salt and 200g of the flour. Beat to a smooth dough that's a similar consistency to shortbread. As soon as you have a smooth paste, stop beating and tip it into the tart tin. With your hands, press the pastry onto the base and up the sides of the tin as evenly as possible. Prick the base repeatedly with a fork, then put in the freezer for 1 hour.

Preheat the oven to 190°C/170°C fan/gas mark 5.

Once the pastry has solidified, line it with a layer of baking paper and fill with baking beans or rice, all the way up to the top of the pastry wall. Bake blind for 15 minutes, remove the beans and paper and then return to the oven for a further 5 minutes. Once the pastry case is baked, remove it from the oven and allow to cool slightly, but leave the oven switched on.

For the filling, cube the remaining 180g of butter and place it into a saucepan with the bay leaves. Heat on low until the butter has entirely melted, then increase the heat to medium–high and allow the butter to brown. It will bubble and spit as the water evaporates, but when it starts to smell like hazelnuts and you have a thick, fine-bubbled foam on top, it's ready. Pour it into a cold bowl and allow to infuse for 5 minutes or so.

Whisk together the remaining 3 eggs and 170g of sugar just until the sugar dissolves. Whisk in the last 100g of flour with a pinch of salt, then slowly incorporate the melted butter as you whisk – the mixture should be velvety and smooth. Remove the bay leaves and pour the filling into the tart case. Dot the blackberries into the filling randomly and scatter over a little extra sugar. Bake the tart for 35–40 minutes, until golden brown, then allow to cool completely in the tin before serving.

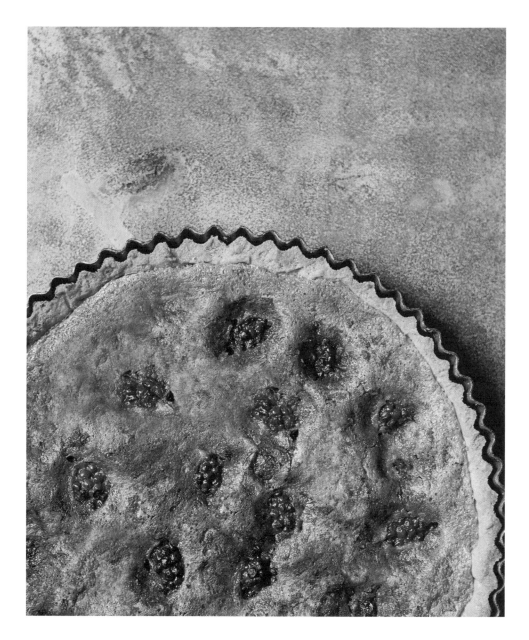

Chocolate Orange Panna Cotta

MAKES
4

I'm always surprised at how many people are afraid to use gelatine. It's as though it would only take one wrong move for the entire kitchen to implode, but it really is such an easy thing to use – especially leaf gelatine. All it needs is 5 minutes or so soaking in cold water and then it can be dissolved in a hot liquid.

These creamy little puddings are as easy to make as they are delicious to devour, and I just can't resist how they tremble ever so slightly when nudged.

220g dark chocolate (60% cocoa solds)

2 gelatine leaves

475ml single cream

1 teaspoon orange extract

100g white chocolate

Have 4 × 180ml pudding moulds at the ready – or use ramekins or mugs.

Roughly chop the chocolate and put it into a heatproof bowl. Submerge the gelatine leaves in a bowl of cold water and leave them to bloom – basically they go from being stiff to soft and floppy.

In a saucepan, bring the cream to a simmer. Once it is simmering, add the orange extract and remove the pan from the heat. Squeeze the excess moisture out of the gelatine leaves, add them to the cream and stir until they dissolve. Pour the hot cream over the chocolate and leave it for 30 seconds to melt before stirring everything together into a smooth, glossy liquid.

Divide the mixture between the pudding moulds, allow to cool to room temperature, then cover with cling film and refrigerate for at least 4 hours, though overnight is best.

If you want to turn out the panna cotta, dunk each mould into a bowl of boiling water for just a few seconds, to just below the rim, before inverting onto a plate. If the pudding doesn't slip out, give the mould a tap or two on the bottom. If it still won't slip out, run a knife around the edge of the panna cotta and the mould, then try again. And if that fails, don't lose your rag – just eat it out of the mould!

Melt the white chocolate in a heatproof bowl over a pan of barely simmering water – don't let the bottom of the bowl touch the water – and drizzle it over the panna cotta.

Lemon and Rosemary Almond Cake

Lemon drizzle cake is one of those cakes that seems to have always been around. There are countless recipes, each with their own twist, but when baked with rosemary it is particularly delicious. I first tried this combination at the E5 Bakehouse in London – theirs was made with polenta – and I just had to make a version of my own.

Because this is made with ground almonds, it's gluten-free, too. And in the event that there are leftovers (as if!), it will last a good week or so in an airtight tin.

Preheat the oven to 170°C/150°C fan/gas mark 3. Grease and line with baking paper a 23cm loose-bottomed cake tin.

Separate 5 of the eggs, placing the whites into one bowl and the yolks into another. Put the remaining whole egg into the bowl with the yolks and add 300g of the sugar and the zest of all 3 lemons. Whisk the yolks and sugar until the sugar more or less dissolves into the yolks, then beat in the almonds. This will be an almost impossibly thick batter, but that is normal.

Using a clean whisk, whisk the egg whites to fairly stiff peaks. Scoop one third of the egg white into the yolk mixture and beat vigorously to slacken. Gently fold the remaining egg white into the batter using a spatula or large metal spoon, being careful not to deflate the whites. Pour the batter into the prepared cake tin and bake for 45–50 minutes, until a skewer inserted into the centre comes out fairly clean – there may be the odd moist crumb on there, but that's fine.

While the cake bakes, make the syrup. Put the remaining sugar into a saucepan with the juice of all 3 lemons, the water and the rosemary sprigs. Bring to the boil, stirring. Boil for 1 minute, then set aside until the cake is baked.

As soon as the baked cake comes out of the oven, stab it repeatedly with a skewer, then pour the syrup over the top and leave it to soak in while the cake cools completely, in the tin.

SERVES 8

6 large eggs

400g caster sugar

3 large unwaxed lemons

300g ground almonds

2 sprigs of rosemary

50ml water

Secret Ingredient Chocolate Fudge Cake

SERVES
10–12

Here is a recipe that I just know some purist folk will scoff at but, believe me, this is not a new way of making the densest, most fudgy chocolate cake imaginable. The secret is condensed tomato soup. In fact, chocolate cake made with this special ingredient was one of Sylvia Plath's favourite bakes, and I can honestly see why. The result is so flavoursome and rich; somehow the tomato soup enhances both flavour and texture. It's my new favourite chocolate cake, and one I think is impossible to compete with.

640g dark brown muscovado sugar

220g can condensed cream of tomato soup

4 large eggs

320g self-raising flour

230g cocoa powder

240g unsalted butter, softened, plus extra for greasing
390ml boiled water

Preheat the oven to 180°C/160°C fan/gas mark 4. Grease two 20cm sandwich tins – preferably loose-bottomed – and line the bases with neatly cut circles of baking paper.

I make the batter in a freestanding electric mixer fitted with the paddle attachment, but you could make it with a handheld electric beater and mixing bowl. Cream 120g of the butter with 400g of the sugar and half the tomato soup – you want to try to break down the sugar as best you can and get it pretty much entirely dissolved. Add the remaining soup and beat that in, along with the eggs. If the batter looks split here, that's nothing to worry about, just carry on.

Sift the flour and 80g of the cocoa powder over the batter and beat in, then add 240ml of the boiled water in a steady thin stream whilst beating. As soon as you have a velvety smooth cake batter, divide between the two cake tins and bake for 25–35 minutes, or until a skewer inserted into the centre of each cake comes out clean. The cakes may crack on top, but don't worry at all. Allow to cool for 5 minutes in the tin, then invert onto a wire rack to finish cooling.

While the cakes are baking, make the icing. Place the remaining ingredients (150ml water, 240g sugar, 150g cocoa and 120g butter) into a saucepan and heat over a medium heat, stirring constantly. As soon as everything melts together and the sugar is dissolved, remove from the heat. Allow to cool in the pan.

Once the cakes are cool and the chocolate icing is a thick, spreadable consistency, it's time to ice. Take one cake, place it onto a cake stand or plate and spread roughly a third of the icing over the top. Place the other cake on top – I always put it on upside down to get a flat top. Spread the remaining icing over the top and sides of the cake – a small palette knife is the best tool for this, but the back of a tablespoon would work in emergency situations.

Variation

A light brown muscovado sugar would work if that's all you have, but I'd steer clear of using caster. The darker, wetter sugars add to the fudgy qualities of the cake. And I probably don't need to warn you against the herby varieties of soup…

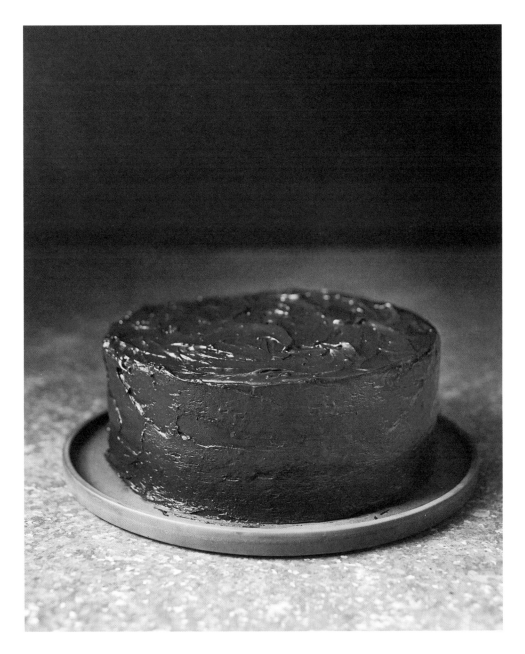

Nutella Pudding with Caramelised Pretzels

MAKES
6

The real trickery in this pudding is that you can make it with just two ingredients, Nutella and eggs. This isn't my original idea: social media went mad for Nutella cake back in 2012, but I wondered what would happen if I whisked the egg whites before adding them. The result was an inelegant soufflé, and inelegant – but delicious – it shall stay.

75g caster sugar

150g salted pretzels

---

6 large eggs

450g Nutella

150ml double cream

Preheat the oven to 200°C/180°C fan/gas mark 6. Have six 175ml (approx.) ramekins or pudding moulds at the ready, but don't grease them. Have a sheet of baking paper ready to tip the caramelised pretzels onto.

First get the caramelised pretzels done. Heat a saucepan over a medium-high heat and, once it's hot, add the sugar. Allow the sugar to melt and turn into a caramel – you can stir it as it melts. If you find there are a few lumps of sugar, remove the pan from the heat as you stir those until dissolved. As soon as you have a golden caramel, add the pretzels and stir to coat, then tip out onto the sheet of baking paper and allow to cool completely.

Separate the eggs, putting the whites into one mixing bowl and the yolks into another. Add the Nutella to the bowl with the yolks and beat vigorously until smooth – this is far easier with a handheld electric whisk.

Whisk the egg whites in their bowl until stiff and cloud-like. Add a third of the egg white to the Nutella mixture and beat in to slacken, then add the remaining egg white and fold in gently, until completely incorporated. Divide the mixture between the ramekins, filling them completely, then bake in the oven for 20-25 minutes. You can take these out when they're still slightly runny in the centre, but I prefer them completely baked and brownie-like. And don't worry that these rise and crack on top, it is part of their rustic charm.

Whisk the cream to soft, floppy peaks and spoon that over the puddings – it probably won't all fit on in one go, but I like to add more as I eat. Roughly chop the caramelised pretzels and scatter them over the top of the cream.

Coconut Macaroon and Lime Cheesecake

**SERVES
10**

On one of my particularly greedy afternoons, I was nibbling on a batch of – admittedly, shop-bought – coconut macaroons, and thought they were a little dry. I raided the fridge and found cream cheese and lime curd, so I put them both to good use. The idea for this came instantly, and the next day I had to get down to work. The trick to an utterly toothsome macaroon base is to combine the coconut with melted marshmallows before baking. And since marshmallows are a great setting agent, I used them for the filling, too, so there is no need to bake it.

360g white mini marshmallows

300g desiccated coconut

300g good-quality lime curd

450g full-fat cream cheese

Zest of 1 lime

2 tablespoons water

Preheat the oven to 180°C/160°C fan/gas mark 4. Grease and line the base and sides of a 23cm springform cake tin.

For the coconut macaroon base, put 180g of the marshmallows into a heatproof bowl with 1 tablespoon of the water. Set over a pan of barely simmering water and stir until the marshmallows melt into a thick goo. Add the coconut – still over the heat – and stir until well coated in the marshmallow melt. Tip into the cake tin and press it over the base and up the sides. I find it far easier when I grease my hands with a little oil, and I prefer a more rustic, uneven edge (see picture). Bake the base in the oven for 15 minutes, until golden brown. This will puff up a little, so as soon as it comes out of the oven, press it down gently to compact it. Allow to cool.

For the filling, repeat the marshmallow melting process with the remaining 180g marshmallows and the remaining tablespoon of water. Once melted, remove from the heat and beat in the lime curd, then beat in the cream cheese – it's easier to do this with a whisk but don't whisk to aerate, just vigorously mix until smooth. Pour the filling into the cooled coconut base and refrigerate overnight. Don't be impatiently prodding this or prematurely slicing it; just forget about it until it sets completely. Sprinkle over the lime zest before serving.

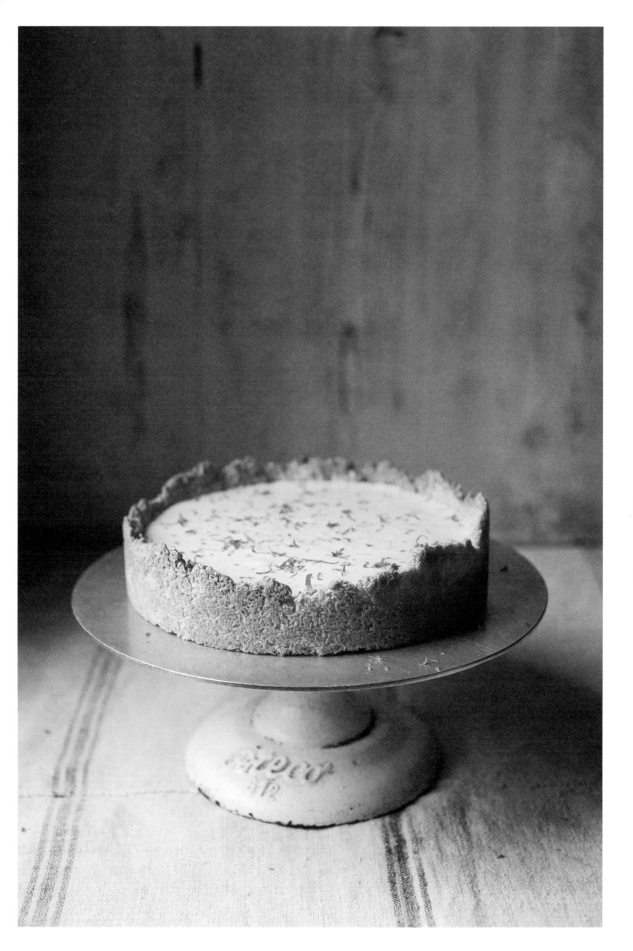

Mont Blanc Triangle Torte

SERVES
8-10

This is my abstract version of Mont Blanc – both mountain and dessert. The flavour combination makes up the classic French dish, while the form of this triangular, meringue-covered torte represents a snow-topped mountain range. You may think I've made a mistake in using plain flour instead of self-raising, but that is a purposeful selection; if this were an aerated cake mixture it would be far more difficult to cut and shape.

185g caster sugar

---

3 large eggs

110g plain flour

15g cocoa powder,
plus extra for dusting

250g can sweetened
chestnut spread
(I use the Clément
Faugier vanilla variety)

125g unsalted butter,
at room temperature,
plus extra for greasing

Preheat the oven to 200°C/180°C fan/gas mark 6. Grease a 33 × 23cm Swiss roll tin and line the base with baking paper.

Beat the butter until pale and fluffy, either with a handheld electric whisk or using a freestanding electric mixer fitted with the paddle attachment. Add 125g of the sugar and stir through to avoid causing a giant cloud of sweet sugar smoke, then beat until well incorporated. Beat in 2 of the eggs until well blended, then beat in the flour and cocoa powder until you have a smooth batter.

Scoop the batter into the Swiss roll tin, level off and bake for 12–15 minutes, or until a skewer comes out clean. Remove from the oven and allow to cool completely in the tin.

Take the torte from the tin and place it horizontally on the worktop before you, then slice it into 4 equal rectangles – I cut it in half, then cut each half in half.

Spread a quarter of the chestnut spread over one of the torte rectangles. Place another rectangle evenly on top, then repeat until you have four layers of torte sandwiched together with three layers of filling. Don't worry if the edges don't line up perfectly at this stage. Place into the freezer for 20 minutes to firm up.

When the torte is chilled and firm, take it out of the freezer and carefully trim all four edges to neaten. Place the torte on the worktop with the layers lying horizontally. With great care and a sharp serrated bread knife, slice the torte in half on a diagonal into two long triangular pieces. I place one of the longer edges of the torte at the edge of the worktop, then I position the blade of my knife on the right hand side of the torte, from the bottom corner (the one nearest to me) to top corner (the one furthest away from me). Using the edge of the worktop to guide the knife, I gently saw the torte in half. If you're left-handed, start at the left-hand side and saw the knife towards the right.

Align the pieces so that the backs are touching and the stripes of torte are vertical. Spread the remaining chestnut spread on the back of one of the triangles and then stick them together. Chill again for another 20 minutes.

Separate the remaining egg – you can freeze the yolk to use at a later date – and place the white with the remaining 60g of sugar into a heatproof mixing bowl. Set the bowl over a pan of barely simmering water and, using a handheld electric beater, whisk until the mixture feels slightly hot and the sugar has dissolved into the egg white. Remove from the heat, but keep whisking until you have a very thick, smooth and glossy meringue.

Spread the meringue over the sloping sides of the torte and sprinkle over a light dusting of cocoa powder.

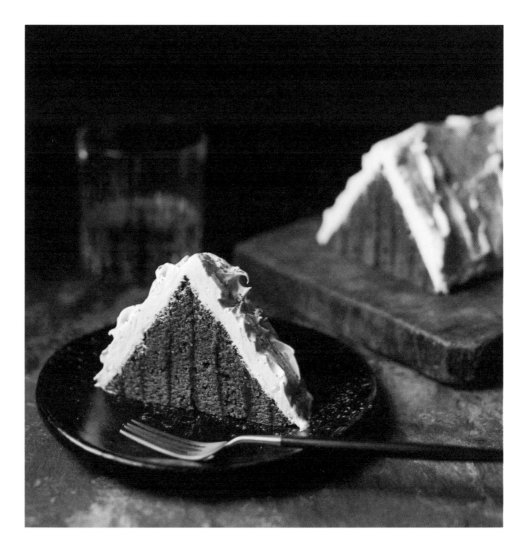

Autumnal Apple Crisp Cake

SERVES
10–12

This cake makes an impression, but rest assured that because precision isn't required when it comes to decorating it, the more rustic the Swiss meringue is, the better the cake will look. It does take a little time to get all of the different elements ready, but an afternoon off, dedicated to baking, is never a wasteful occupation.

720g caster sugar

4 Braeburn apples

11 large eggs

340g self-raising flour

3 tablespoons
mixed spice, plus
extra for dusting

100ml water
340g unsalted butter,
at room temperature

Preheat the oven to 130°C/110°C fan/gas mark ½.

Combine 100ml water with 100g of the sugar in a saucepan and bring to the boil. Boil for 1 minute, then turn off the heat. Slice 2 of the apples finely, using a mandoline – there's no need to peel or core them. Dip the slices into the hot syrup and leave to soak for 1 minute, then remove and allow the syrup to drip off them – I lay them on a cooling rack set over a couple of pieces of kitchen paper to drip dry, just for a minute or two.

Arrange the apple slices, well spaced, on 2 baking sheets lined with baking paper. Put into the oven and leave to dry out for 2 hours, flipping the apple slices over after 1 hour. Remove the slices from the oven, arrange them on a dry cooling rack and leave them to cool and crisp completely.

Increase the oven temperature to 180°C/160°C fan/gas mark 4. Grease three 20cm sandwich tins, preferably loose-bottomed, and line the bases with neatly cut circles of baking paper.

Beat the butter with 340g of the sugar until well creamed and fluffy. Add 6 of the eggs, one at a time, beating well after each addition, then add the flour and mixed spice and beat until smooth. Peel and core the remaining 2 apples, chop them into small dice and fold them through the batter.

Divide the batter between the cake tins as evenly as possible, smooth out the tops with the back of a spoon and bake for 30–35 minutes, or until a skewer inserted into the centre comes out clean. Remove from the oven and allow to cool in the tins for 5 minutes, then invert onto wire racks to cool completely.

For the meringue, separate the remaining 5 eggs and place the whites into a heatproof bowl along with the remaining 280g sugar – freeze the yolks for another time. Set the bowl over a pan of barely simmering water and whisk with a handheld electric mixer until the mixture feels slightly warm on the finger. Remove the bowl from the pan and continue whisking until you have a very thick, smooth meringue.

To assemble, simply place one cake onto a cake stand and spread over some of the meringue. Repeat until you have three layers of cake sandwiched together with two layers of meringue. Spread the remaining meringue over the top and sides of the cake, scraping the meringue away to reveal the sponge layers. Finish the cake by placing the apple slices around the base, then sprinkle over a little mixed spice. If you have a chef's blowtorch you can char the meringue slightly, but it's just as beautiful without.

Self-saucing Orange Curd Pudding

There's something almost miraculous about a self-saucing pudding: you just throw all of the ingredients together and it comes out cosily warm and soaked in a thick, sweet sauce. If you wanted to prepare this in advance, you could. Just make the batter and pour it into the dish, then refrigerate until required – for no more than 2 days, though. Make the sauce fresh and pour that over the pudding just before baking.

SERVES
8

Preheat the oven to 180°C/160°C fan/gas mark 4. Grease a 30 × 20cm pudding tray.

For the batter, beat the butter, 150ml water, 150g of the orange curd, 250g of the sugar, the flour, eggs and grated zest of the oranges until smooth – I do this in a food processor, but a freestanding mixer works fine, as would a wooden spoon and elbow grease. Pour the batter into the prepared tray and refrigerate for 1 hour.

For the sauce, whisk together the remaining 300g of orange curd with 175ml boiling water and the remaining 50g of sugar with the juice of 1 of the oranges. Pour the sauce over the pudding then bake for 50–60 minutes, or until a skewer inserted into the centre comes out clean. Do bear in mind there is sauce in this pudding, which will stick to the skewer. Leave to stand for 10 minutes before you dig in.

450g orange curd

300g light brown muscovado sugar

300g self-raising flour

2 large eggs

2 oranges

175g unsalted butter, softened, plus extra for greasing
325ml water, 150ml at room temperature, 175ml boiling

Brown-sugar Meringues with Hazelnut Butterscotch Sauce

MAKES
4

Meringues have been done time and time again, but with very good reason: they're delicious. Nothing quite compares to that crispy outer shell, beneath which lies a pillowy marshmallow centre. I remember my mum experimenting with brown sugar in a meringue once, and the result was so chewy and beautifully flavoured. Dark muscovado sugar is somewhat damper than regular caster, so this recipe uses a Swiss meringue method, the result of which is a little more stable than the usual French meringue.

---

4 large egg whites

275g dark brown muscovado sugar

10g cocoa powder

40g hazelnuts

250ml double cream

50g unsalted butter

Preheat the oven to 160°C/140°C fan/gas mark 3. Line two baking sheets with baking paper.

Put the egg whites into a heatproof mixing bowl and add 225g of the sugar. Set the bowl over a pan of barely simmering water and whisk – this is more easily done using a handheld electric mixer. Whisking constantly, allow the sugar to dissolve, and as soon as the mixture feels slightly hot on the finger, remove from the heat and whisk vigorously until you have a very smooth, stiff meringue – a good 5 minutes or so. Blob 4 large piles of meringue, well spaced, onto the baking sheets and with the back of a spoon morph them into little indented nests. Sprinkle over the cocoa powder and put the meringues into the oven, reducing the heat to 140°C/120°C fan/gas mark 1. Bake for 2 hours, then turn off the oven and open the door slightly, to allow the meringues to cool and crisp inside.

Heat a dry frying pan over a high heat, then toss the hazelnuts in the pan for a minute or so, just until gently toasted; they should smell of hazelnuts, but not bitterly so. Chop the toasted nuts roughly and put them into a bowl.

For the sauce, put the remaining 50g of sugar into a saucepan with the butter and 50ml of the double cream. Bring to the boil, stirring, and as soon as it's velvety smooth and well mixed, remove from the heat.

To serve, whisk the remaining 200ml of double cream until soft and floppy. Spoon the cream over the meringues, then drizzle over the sauce and scatter over the toasted hazelnuts.

Sticky Toffee Pudding Banana Upside-down Cake

SERVES
8–10

I know the name is a mouthful, but I don't think there's another way to describe the sheer decadent indulgence of this. And besides, it really is a hybrid of those two things: the soaked dates are based on the classic sticky toffee pudding, but I treat it like an upside-down cake with the caramelised banana slices.

Now – pay attention here; this is important – when this first comes out of the oven and cools, it's a little dry. It must be made the day before eating. I realise that's a big ask, but your patience will pay off.

Finely chop the dates and put them into a heatproof bowl with a pinch of salt and the boiling water. Leave to soak for a good 30 minutes.

Preheat the oven to 180°C/160°C fan/gas mark 4. Grease and line a 20cm square cake tin.

Sprinkle 50g of the sugar over the base of the cake tin, then slice 3 of the bananas in half lengthways and line these up, cut-side down, on top of the sugar.

Mash the remaining banana, then beat it together with the butter, the remaining sugar, the eggs, flour, dates and their soaking water – there's really no need to do this in stages, just get it beaten. Once you have a smooth batter, pour it into the tin over the bananas, level out with a spatula or the back of a spoon, then bake for 45–55 minutes. You'll know it is baked when a skewer inserted into the centre of the cake comes out clean.

Allow the cake to cool in the tin for just 5 minutes, then invert onto a wire rack and allow to cool completely – you might need to run a knife between the edge of the cake and the tin to release it. Peel off the baking paper, being careful not to dislodge the bananas. As soon as the cake is cool, wrap it in cling film or put into an airtight container and, please, just try to forget about it until tomorrow.

120g pitted dates

220g light brown muscovado sugar

4 ripe bananas

2 large eggs

200g self-raising flour

Sea salt flakes
120ml boiling water
145g unsalted butter

Hodgepodge Doughnut Pudding

SERVES
6-8

This is really just a bread and butter pudding made with filled doughnuts, but I call it 'hodgepodge' simply because I like to use a range of different, but complementary, doughnuts. The choice is, of course, yours. Particular favourites of mine are blueberry jam doughnuts mixed with apple and cinnamon.

This could easily be made the night before, then quickly cooked off when required, saving you time.

---

12 mixed filled
doughnuts

300ml full-fat milk

300ml double cream,
plus extra for serving

---

3 large eggs

---

3 tablespoons
demerara sugar

Butter, softened
for greasing

Grease a medium-sized roasting tray or pie dish with butter. Cut the doughnuts into quarters and scatter, randomly, into the dish.

Beat together the milk, cream and eggs until well combined and pour this mixture over the doughnuts. Leave the custard to soak into the doughnuts for a good 30 minutes. Meanwhile, preheat the oven to 180°C/160°C fan/gas mark 4.

Once the doughnuts have soaked up some of the custard, scatter over the demerara sugar and bake for 40–50 minutes, until golden brown and ever so slightly wobbly. Allow to cool slightly before serving with lashings of cream.

Index

Index